CULTURES OF THE WORLD

Czech Republic

Cavendish
Square
New York

Published in 2019 by Cavendish Square Publishing, LLC
243 5th Avenue, Suite 136, New York, NY 10016
Copyright © 2019 by Cavendish Square Publishing, LLC
Third Edition

Library of Congress Cataloging-in-Publication Data

Names: Sioras, Efstathia, author. | Spilling, Michael, author. | Nevins, Debbie, author.
Title: Czech Republic / Efstathia Sioras, Michael Spilling, Debbie Nevins.
Description: Third edition. | New York : Cavendish Square, 2018. | Series: Cultures of the world | Includes bibliographical references and index.
Identifiers: LCCN 2018000509 (print) | LCCN 2018001384 (ebook) | ISBN 9781502636379 (eBook) | ISBN 9781502636362 (library bound)
Subjects: LCSH: Czech Republic--Juvenile literature.
Classification: LCC DB2065 (ebook) | LCC DB2065 .S56 2018 (print) | DDC 943.71--dc23
LC record available at https://lccn.loc.gov/2018000509

Writers, Efstathia Sioras, Michael Spilling; Debbie Nevins, third edition
Editorial Director, third edition: David McNamara
Editor, third edition: Debbie Nevins
Art Director, third edition: Amy Greenan
Designer, third edition: Jessica Nevins
Picture Researcher, third edition: Jessica Nevins

PRECEDING PAGE
The Church of Our Lady before Týn is a landmark in Old Town Square in Prague.

Printed in the United States of America

CONTENTS

CZECH REPUBLIC TODAY

LOCATED IN CENTRAL EUROPE, THE CZECH (CHEK) REPUBLIC IS QUITE A NEW nation. It was formed after the nonviolent breakup of the former Czechoslovakia in 1993. The Czechs and the Slovaks who had been citizens of that conjoined nation since its founding in 1918 were eager to part ways. So they divvied up the land and the Czechs formed their own country in the western part of it, while the Slovaks formed theirs—the Slovak Republic—in the south and east. The breakup has famously been called the Velvet Divorce—"velvet" because it occurred without war and bloodshed, a truly rare occurrence in the history of the world's nations.

The Czech Republic (*Ceska Republika* in the Czech language) must have seemed too long for everyday use to its people, who call it *Cesko* for short. Many countries have shortened versions of their names; for example, the Slovak Republic is more commonly called Slovakia. For English speakers, however, the Czech Republic went without a shortened name until 2016, when the government decided on Czechia (CHECK-iya). While some media and information sources, including the United Nations and the International Organization for Standardization, immediately adopted the new name—others have been slower to follow. Google Maps and the

CIA World Factbook have switched to Czechia; while the *Encyclopedia Britannica* sticks, for the most part, with the Czech Republic. After all, the Czech Republic remains the nation's official, formal name and therefore is not incorrect. Czechia is not to be confused with Chechnya, also known as the Chechen Republic, which is a whole other place—a part of Russia.

Both inside and outside the Czech Republic, the new name caused some consternation. People found it hard to say or assumed it was a made-up name. But apparently the name Czechia dates to 1569 in Latin and was used occasionally in English language media in the nineteenth and twentieth centuries in reference to the western part of Czechoslovakia. Proponents of the new name reject the claim that it sounds odd and argue that the world will get used to it. So, while the English-speaking world adapts to the country's new informal name, this book will use the Czech Republic most of the time, with occasional references to Czechia.

Far from the sea in any direction, the Czech Republic is a land-locked country surrounded by mountains. Its neighbors are, clockwise from the north, Poland to the northeast, Slovakia to the southeast, Austria to the south, and Germany surrounding it on the west. Often called the "Land of Castles," Czechia boasts more old castles than any other country, and Prague Castle, in the capital city, is certified by the *Guinness Book of World Records* to be the largest in the world.

The Czech countryside is dominated by forests, hills, and mountains, which along with its many castles give it an air of enchantment, or so say the tourist websites. And many visitors are indeed charmed by the beautiful land. Many Czech cities and towns have well-preserved historical building sites ranging from medieval squares to Baroque churches.

Prague, the capital, is the nation's jewel. The "City of a Hundred Spires" is dense with churches, cathedrals, castles, and a wide range of remarkable architecture. It's not a huge city—it's the fourteenth-largest in the European Union—but it is one of the most visually impressive. The red-roofed city on the Vltava River has long been called "the handsomest city in Europe," and it continues to top lists of Europe's "most beautiful" cities, giving Paris tough competition.

In addition to its historic buildings, Prague is a cultural center, particularly for lovers of classical music. The Czech Republic was home to Smetana, Dvořák, and Janáček—composers who, like Beethoven, Mozart, and Tchaikovsky, need only their famous last names to evoke awe and delight worldwide. But fans of jazz, rock, pop, rap, and other forms of music can find plenty dance halls, concert venues, and laid-back cafes to enjoy as well in this thoroughly modern city. Prague is also the proud home of the world's largest Lego Museum.

Tempting as it may be to paint the country as a kind of fairyland, the Czech Republic has not enjoyed an enchanted history. It spent most of the twentieth century as part of Czechoslovakia, in somewhat different forms, with parts or all of it annexed, occupied, lopped off, or re-established at various times throughout the century. It spent several years under the yoke of Nazi Germany, and then as a satellite country of the Soviet Union.

MLÉČNÁ JÍDELNA

Graffiti on a building in Prague announces victory in the Velvet Revolution.

Under Communist rule, the country's economy stagnated, the people grew disillusioned, and a dissident movement arose.

In 1989, at a time when Communist governments were falling like dominoes across Eastern Europe, and the Soviet Union itself was coming apart at its seams, Czechs staged the "Velvet Revolution" and restored Czechoslovakia to democracy. Soon after, in 1993, the country peacefully dissolved itself, forming two new countries. Today, the Czech Republic is a thriving free nation with an economy growing ever stronger—and the rest, as they say, is history.

Except—the real story is far more complex. It is true that the new Czech nation has been growing stronger economically and has enjoyed more than two decades of peace. Eager to align itself with the West, the Czech Republic joined the North Atlantic Treaty Organization (NATO) in 1999 and the European Union (EU) in 2004. But the fairytale ending many had hoped for has not come to pass. Some say Western Europe was slow to accommodate or welcome its newly democratic Eastern neighbors. Whatever the reasons, Czechs who expected a worry-free life of wealth and ease were surprised to find that democracy isn't easy and is certainly not a panacea to any country's woes.

Forty years of Communism left its mark, and the Czech people are profoundly distrustful of one another, of strangers, and of the government. Although they are generally happy and successful in many ways, they are nevertheless feeling grumpy these days. And they are afraid of terrorism, which has been on the rise in Europe. According to a recent poll, 68 percent of Czech respondents said attacks in Europe by the Islamic State terror organization was the number one threat to their country. An additional 25 percent said the danger was "relatively serious." Second on the list of threats was the impact of wars in Syria, Africa, and Asia—which have prompted vast waves of migrants to flood into Europe. The Czech's third-greatest fear, according to this poll, was the escalation of conflicts between Russia and Eastern Europe—such as in Ukraine, the Baltic States, and Georgia.

Perhaps for these reasons, xenophobic populism has been on the rise in the Czech Republic (and elsewhere in Europe and the United States). In 2013, the Czechs elected a president, Miloš Zeman, who is known for his hardline anti-Islam rhetoric. And in 2017, they chose as their prime minister Andrej Babiš—a billionaire businessman with a shady past who has been compared to Donald Trump. As far-right politics and nationalist rhetoric is gaining traction in Czechia, with leaders talking about building walls to keep out illegal migrants, the international community, and the European Union in particular, is watching with no small amount of concern.

GEOGRAPHY

An aerial shot shows the Hrubá Skála Castle in the Liberec Region of the Czech Republic.

1

LOCATED IN CENTRAL EUROPE, THE Czech Republic is a landlocked country. Far from the seas, it is nevertheless blessed with an abundance of rivers and streams, which flow down from its mountainous landscapes.

Until 1992, it was part of a larger country. Slovakia and the Czech Republic together made up the nation of Czechoslovakia, founded in 1918. Today, the Czech Republic (Czechia) borders the Slovak Republic

POLAND

Liberec

Karlovy Vary

Elbe

PRAGUE ●

Hradec Králové

Plzeň ●

Kutná Hora

Ostrava

CZECH REPUBLIC

Brno

České Budějovice

Český Krumlov

GERMANY

AUSTRIA

SLOVAKIA

This map shows the Czech Republic, its major cities, and its surrounding neighbors.

With more than two thousand castles and keeps (fortified towers), the Czech Republic is sometimes called the "castle capital of the world." The St. Vitus Cathedral at Prague Castle is home to the Czech crown jewels and the burial place of Czech kings. Dating from the ninth century, the Prague Castle complex in the capital city now contains the residence and offices of the nation's president.

The Elbe River is little more than a stream in the early part of its journey, in Krkonoše National Park in the Czech Republic.

(Slovakia) to the east and southeast. Czechia also shares borders with Austria to the south, Germany to the north and west, and Poland to the north. It is slightly smaller than South Carolina in the United States.

The country's geography is made up of agricultural land and forests. Continuous forest belts border the mountains, while the lowlands have traditionally been developed for agricultural uses. Although large areas of original forest have been cleared for cultivation and for timber, thick woodlands remain a dominant feature of the Czech landscape.

The republic's scenery varies dramatically from limestone caves and natural springs to beautiful mountain ranges and numerous rivers. Cities and towns are well distributed throughout the land.

BOHEMIA TO THE WEST

The Czech Republic consists of two major regions: Bohemia to the west and Moravia to the east. Their landscapes differ; Bohemia is essentially a 1,640 foot (500 meter) high plateau surrounded by low mountains, while Moravia, particularly east Moravia, is hilly.

BOHEMIAN SWITZERLAND

A particularly pretty and geologically unusual part of the Czech Republic is a region in the northwest called České Švýcarsko, or Czech Switzerland. Popularly also known as Bohemian Switzerland (and Saxon Switzerland in Germany), the picturesque landscape is craggy and mountainous—a place of high cliffs and deep gorges.

The Elbe River runs through the region, crossing from Bohemia in the Czech Republic to Saxony in southeastern Germany on its way to the North Sea. In this region, it winds its way through the Elbe Sandstone Mountains, a part of the mountain chain that includes the Ore Mountains to the west and the Lusatian Mountains to the east.

Pravčická brána (bránā means "gate"), a natural sandstone arch—the largest in Europe—is found in this region, along with many other strange rock formations. The mysterious and fantastical landscape has attracted artists, poets, composers, and other creative folks for centuries. Even the nineteenth-century fairytale writer Hans Christian Andersen found inspiration here. More recently, the 2005 movie The Chronicles of Narnia: The Lion, The Witch, and the Wardrobe *was partly filmed in Bohemian Switzerland, and included shots of the sandstone arch.*

In 2000, the Czech Republic's newest national park was established to protect the natural wilderness of the area. The České Švýcarsko National Park encompasses the forests, the rocky landscapes, and the sandstone arch, as well as Růžovský vrch (vrch mean "hill"), the region's dominant mountain, and Soutěsky Kamenice (Kamnitz Gorge).

The Pravčická brána rock formation is a feature of České Švýcarsko.

The confluence of the Vltava and Elbe rivers in Melnik, Czech Republic.

Bohemia is drained by the Elbe River (also called the Labe River), which provides access to the North Sea. Its tributary, the Vltava River (also called the Moldau River), at 270 miles (435 km), is the longest river in the Czech Republic. The region's chief towns are Prague, Plzeň (called Pilsen in English), and České Budějovice.

Providing natural frontiers for Bohemia are the Šumava Mountains to the southwest, the Ore Mountains to the northwest (forming the border with Germany), the Riesengebirge (also called the Krkonoše or Giant) Mountains along the Polish border to the northeast, and the Bohemian-Moravian Highlands that divide Bohemia and Moravia. Mount Sněžka (5,256 feet/1,602 m) is the highest mountain in the republic and is part of the Giant Mountain range.

Bohemia is subdivided into five areas: North, South, East, West, and Central Bohemia. The topography of South Bohemia is unusual. Since the sixteenth century, the land around the city of České Budějovice has been gradually sculpted into a network of hundreds of linked fishponds and artificial lakes. Today they are used to farm-raise carp, a popular Christmas fish dish in Bohemia.

The republic's largest artificial lake is also located in the south, near Třeboň: Lake Rožmberk was created in 1590 and covers about 1,235 acres (500 hectares). The republic's other large body of water is the lake behind Lipno Dam, near the Austrian border.

North Bohemia has long been the most highly industrialized region of the Czech Republic. Because it is the site of extensive coal and iron ore mining, North Bohemia has suffered severe air pollution. Over the last decade, however, there has been an enormous effort to improve the whole environment and the quality of the region's air. Today, people in parts of North Bohemia breathe a cleaner air and enjoy a greener landscape than in the recent past.

MORAVIA TO THE EAST

Essentially lowland, Moravia is also surrounded by mountains: to the west the Bohemian-Moravian Highlands, to the east the White Carpathian and the Javorníky mountains, and to the north the Jeseníky Mountains. Moravia's chief cities are Ostrava and Brno. Moravia is divided into North and South Moravia. In northeast Moravia, there is also a historical region named Silesia. It was a Polish province that was passed to Bohemia in 1335 and taken by Prussia in 1742. Most of Silesia was returned to Poland in 1945; the rest forms part of Germany and the Czech Republic.

The two main rivers in this region are the Morava River, which flows south to the Danube and eventually drains into the Black Sea, and the Oder (also called Odra) River, which courses around the eastern end of the Sudeten Range into Poland and drains into the Baltic Sea. The Oder River caused extensive flooding in mid-1997: a third of the republic was flooded for ten days. More than forty people died, 2,500 were injured, and 10,000 became homeless. Because of the devastation of the agricultural land, the republic had to import enormous amounts of grain to prevent a food shortage.

In the southwest, just north of the city of Brno, lies the wooded highland area called the Moravian Karst, where limestone hills have been carved into canyons and hundreds of caves. Over millions of years, mildly acidic rainwater has seeped through the limestone rock, slowly dissolving sections of it. This has resulted in cave formations filled with colorful stalactites and stalagmites.

South Moravia is renowned for its wineries, which export some excellent wines. This area also produces some fiery plum and apricot brandies, the favorite distilled alcoholic beverages of the Czechs.

RIVERS

There are three principal river systems in the Czech Republic: the Elbe, Oder, and Morava rivers and their tributaries. The country's rivers flow to three different seas: those in southern Moravia flow to the Danube and onward to the Black Sea, the Elbe flows to the North Sea, and the Oder to the Baltic Sea.

The journeys these rivers make are long—the Black Sea is 466 miles (750 km) to the southeast, the North Sea is 329 miles (530 km) to the northwest, and the Baltic Sea is 217 miles (350 km) to the north.

A VARIABLE CLIMATE

The Czech Republic has a temperate continental climate. There are four distinct seasons, including hot, wet summers and cold, drier winters. Temperature and rainfall fluctuate greatly because of variable air pressure—the republic is known for its changeable weather.

In Moravia there is a wide variation in temperature between winter and summer, and day and night, whereas Bohemia receives the moderating influence of an oceanic climate, so day and night temperatures do not vary much. More rain and more frequent cloudy weather are found in Bohemia than in Moravia.

Average summer temperatures range between 70° and 80° Fahrenheit (21° and 27° Celsius). Lowland temperatures often rise above 86°F (30°C). July is the hottest month of the year. In summer it rains, on average, every other day, with hot spells usually broken by heavy thunderstorms. In the highlands temperatures are generally cooler, as they fall with increasing elevation; mountain dwellers often experience near-freezing conditions.

Winter temperatures in the Czech Republic average between 25°F and 28°F (−4°C and −2°C), with January being the coldest month. Temperatures can drop to 5°F (−15°C) in the lowlands, and it can be bitterly cold in the highlands surrounding the Bohemian plateau, where Prague is situated.

Snow and fog are common in the lowlands, with forty to one hundred days of snow in the winter. Typically, there are 130 days of snow in the mountains. The Czech Republic does not have a really dry season. The winter months are slightly drier, with rainfall occurring one day in every three, averaging 20 to 30 inches (50 to 76 centimeters) annually in the lowlands and 32 inches (81 cm) or more in the highlands.

The Czech Republic is located in the main European watershed (the line that divides the drainage basins of the major rivers of Germany). Many Central European rivers originate there. The country's main freshwater source is the precipitation that forms rivers. Rivers are at their highest in the spring and at their lowest in summer. There are also a few freshwater lakes. Most lakes, such as those in southern Bohemia, are man-made and provide a reliable source of fish for local consumption.

FLORA AND FAUNA

The Czech landscape, from agricultural lowlands to steppes and mountain ranges, supports a wide range of vegetation. Despite several hundred years of clear-cutting for cultivation and decades of unregulated industrial development, one-third of the republic is still covered by forest. Deciduous trees such as oaks are found in the lower regions of Moravia. Spruce is common in the lower mountain areas, and beech at higher elevations. Together, beech and spruce forests cover the mountains in the country. Dwarf pine is seen near the tree line. Above the tree line (approximately 4,595 feet/1,400 m), only grasses, shrubs, and lichens thrive.

Two chamois peer at the photographer from the stony landscape of the Lusatian Mountains.

The Czech Republic is rich in fauna. Agricultural practices have allowed certain species, such as hamsters, to sustain large populations. Introduced species have spread rapidly, for example, muskrat, pheasant, and trout. A large variety of wildlife inhabits lower areas of the mountains: bears (almost extinct now), wolves, lynx, foxes, wildcats, marmots, otters, marten, deer, and mink. The chamois, a small mountain antelope hunted for its beautiful coat, came dangerously close to extinction. It is now protected, and its numbers are increasing.

Hunted wildlife common to the woodlands and marshes are hares, rabbits, hamsters, gophers, partridge, pheasant, ducks, and wild geese. Protected species include the large birds: golden eagles, vultures, ospreys, storks, bustards, eagle-owls, and capercaillie (large grouse).

The country's national parks include the Bohemian Forest and the Krkonoše Mountains. The Bohemian Forest is part of an ecotourism project shared by the Czech Republic, Austria, and the state of Bavaria in Germany.

Charles Bridge is an architectural landmark in Prague.

Known as the Green Roof of Europe, this beautiful area attracts tourists who come to enjoy its wildlife as well as outdoor activities such as hiking and cycling.

CITIES

Prior to the industrial revolution, Czechs cultivated the land they lived on. With industrialization, urban areas burgeoned and changed the Czechs' relationship with the land. This has generally resulted in environmental degradation, overcrowding, and a decline in the quality of life.

Because of this deterioration in urban areas, many Czechs purchase vacation homes in the less affected countryside. Farms and old village houses are bought and renovated. This trend has saved much rural architecture that otherwise would have fallen to ruins. However, the construction of new second homes has damaged valuable agricultural land in some areas.

PRAGUE A legend about Prague tells of a princess of a Slav group known as the Czechs, so named after the leader of the group. The girl's name was Libuše. She stood upon a high rock above the river Vltava and uttered the following prophecy: "I see a city whose splendor shall reach the stars." She instructed her people to build a castle on the spot where a man was seen building the threshold of a house. Since the word "threshold" is *prah* in Czech, she asked them to name the castle Praha. Her people carried out her wishes. Two hundred years later, her prophecy came true: the city of Prague (called Praha in Czech) became the seat of the Přemysl dynasty.

Prague is at the geographical middle of Central Bohemia. It has flourished at the heart of Czech history since the Great Bohemian Empire in the ninth century. The republic's longest river, the Vltava, flows through the city. Affectionately named "the city of one hundred spires," Prague displays Romanesque, Gothic, Renaissance, Baroque, and Art Nouveau styles of architecture. Several bridges link the west and east banks of the Vltava, but its landmark bridge is the stone Charles Bridge, begun in 1357 and lined with sculptures, the earliest placed in 1683, and the most recent in 1928.

Prague is organized into several historical districts. On the west bank is the castle district of Hradčany (ha rad CHA nay) with its 1,100-year-old castle and the magnificent fourteenth-century Saint Vitus Cathedral. To its south is the thirteenth century Lesser Quarter, where the workers lived. On the east bank is the Old Town with its central enormous Old Town Square. The New Town, built in the fourteenth century, curves around the Old Town and Wenceslas Square, the site of many political events.

A view of downtown Brno.

Prague is one of Europe's most popular tourist destinations. With a population of around 1.3 million, it is home to a large artistic community spanning the visual and literary arts as well as the music scene.

BRNO This city has a population of around 378,000 and is the second-largest city in the Czech Republic. Dating from the Great Moravian Empire, Brno became the capital of Moravia in the fourteenth century. For many centuries the city remained devoutly Catholic in a mainly Protestant country, eventually becoming Protestant in the late 1500s. During the time of the Austro-Hungarian Empire, it developed a strong textile industry. In 1919 a university was founded in the city. Today Brno is known for the many colorful trade fairs held at the exhibition grounds, the annual motorcycle grand prix, and its international music festival.

OLOMOUC Legend has it that Julius Caesar founded Olomouc. In the eleventh century, after the unification of Bohemia and Moravia, Olomouc became a major seat of administrative power. It was the capital of Moravia for several centuries in the Middle Ages. Today it is home to some 100,000 inhabitants and is the fifth-largest city in the Czech Republic. The town sits

Since 1975, the United Nations Educational, Scientific and Cultural Organization (UNESCO) has maintained a list of international landmarks or regions considered to be of "outstanding value" to the people of the world. Such sites embody the common natural and cultural heritage of humanity, and therefore deserve particular protection. The organization works with the host country to establish plans for managing and conserving their sites. UNESCO also reports on sites which are in imminent or potential danger of destruction and can offer emergency funds to try to save the property.

The organization is continually assessing new sites for inclusion on the World Heritage list. In order to be selected, a site must be of "outstanding universal value" and meet at least one of ten criteria. These required elements include cultural value—that is, artistic, religious, or historical significance—and natural value, including exceptional beauty, unusual natural phenomenon, and scientific importance.

As of 2017, a total of 1073 sites have been listed, including 832 cultural, 206 natural, and 35 mixed properties in 167 nations. The Czech Republic is home to twelve World Heritage sites—quite a large number of sites, for such a small country. Another nineteen sites await consideration on the Tentative List.

All of the confirmed Czech World Heritage sites fall in the cultural category:

- *Gardens and Castle at Kroměříž*
- *Historic Center of Prague*
- *Historic Center of Ceský Krumlov*
- *Historic Center of Telc*
- *Holašovice Historical Village Reservation*
- *Holy Trinity Column in Olomouc*
- *Jewish Quarter and St Procopius' Basilica in Trebic*
- *Kutná Hora: Historical Town Center with the Church of St Barbara and the Cathedral of Our Lady at Sedlec*
- *Lednice-Valtice Cultural Landscape*
- *Litomyšl Castle*
- *Pilgrimage Church of St John of Nepomuk at Zelená Hora*
- *Tugendhat Villa in Brno*

on a gentle bend of the Morava River. A university town, Olomouc displays historical architecture second only to Prague. The town has Baroque-style fountains with classical themes: Hercules, Mercury, Neptune, Jupiter, and imperial founder Caesar. Cobbled streets wind through squares built in the Renaissance, Baroque, and Empire styles.

KARLOVY VARY Situated in the protected Slavkov Forest in the northwest, 1,476 feet (450 m) above sea level, Karlovy Vary (known as Carlsbad in English) is the oldest of the Bohemian spa towns. Its twelve springs are located in or near colonnaded buildings. Folklore claims that King Charles IV was hunting in the nearby woods when a rising jet of hot water scalded his dog. Mineral springs are believed to possess medicinal properties; so Charles IV built a hunting lodge near the biggest spring and gave the town his name, Carlsbad ("Charles's spa"). The health-driven town developed a vibrant cultural life, too. The great poet Goethe visited often, and so did composers Bach, Beethoven, Brahms, Wagner, and Liszt. The annual Dvořák Music Festival attracts many visitors in September, and modern art movements such as Art Nouveau have been centered there. Another significant festival that takes place every summer is the Karlovy Vary International Film Festival.

INTERNET LINKS

http://www.czechtourism.com
This travel site offers photos and information about the cities, attractions, and geographical regions of the Czech Republic.

http://en.czech-unesco.org
The Czech World Heritage Sites are given full coverage, with photos, videos, and virtual tours on this website.

http://whc.unesco.org/en/statesparties/cz
The official UNESCO site includes information, photos, videos about the World Heritage sites and the places on the tentative list.

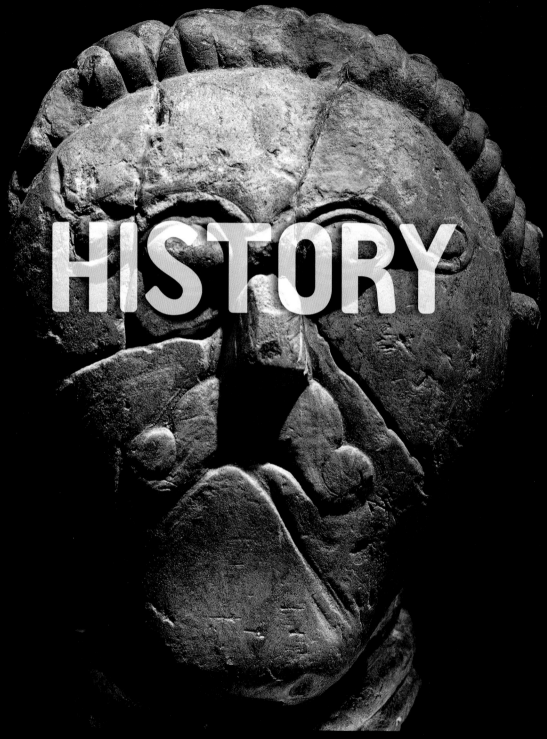

HISTORY

A sculpted stone male head dating from the first or second century BCE is evidence of the Celtic tribes that once lived in Bohemia.

2

THE LAND OF THE CZECH REPUBLIC, or Czechia, has a long history replete with conquests and foreign rule. It has been part of historic empires and ruled by various dynasties, by enlightened leaders and oppressive tyrants. It has been wracked by wars and blessed with periods of peace. Only since January 1, 1993, though, have Czechs enjoyed independent statehood.

EARLY CIVILIZATIONS

Humans inhabited the Czech lands more than six hundred thousand years ago. Evidence exists of established farming communities in the lowlands from approximately 4000 BCE. Tribes of Celtic and Germanic peoples were the first to inhabit the areas that would become Bohemia and Moravia. The Romans named Bohemia after a fifth-century BCE Celtic group, the Boii, or *Boiohemum* in Latin. The Boii were expelled from the region by the Germanic Marcomanni tribe in 8 BCE, but their name remained.

"Life cannot be destroyed for good, neither ... can history be brought entirely to a halt. A secret streamlet trickles on beneath the heavy lid of inertia and pseudo-events, slowly and inconspicuously undercutting it ... (until) the lid will ... start to crack. This is the moment when ... history again demands to be heard." —dissident Václav Havel, 1975, in an open letter to the Communist Czech President Gustáv Husák.

THE GREAT MORAVIAN EMPIRE

By 600 CE, the Slavic ancestors of today's Czechs had settled in the area, calling themselves Moravians, after the Morava River. They united under Mojmír I, who ruled from 830 to 846 CE. Archaeological remains have been discovered in Moravia dating to this period. This Great Moravian Empire included modern-day western Slovakia, Bohemia, Silesia, parts of eastern Germany, southeastern Poland, and northern Hungary.

During the reign of the second ruler of the Moravian Empire, Rostislav, who is also referred to as Rastislav (846—870), the written Slavic language came into existence. At Rostislav's request, the Byzantine emperor in Constantinople sent two monks to introduce Christianity in the region.

The missionaries, Constantine (later renamed Cyril) and his brother, Methodius, arrived in 860 CE. As part of their missionary work in the region, they not only preached in Slavic, but also translated the Bible into the Slavic language then in use. To do this, Cyril created the Slavic alphabet that later developed into the Cyrillic alphabet. Their work was the first example of Slavic in written form.

THE PŘEMYSL DYNASTY

According to tradition, the Přemysl (PRZHE-mysl) dynasty was founded in 800 CE by Přemysl the Ploughman, who started as a humble farm laborer. By 950 CE, the German king Otto I had conquered Bohemia and made it part of the Holy Roman Empire. (The Holy Roman Empire was a union of kingdoms and territories in Central Europe during the early Middle Ages under the rule of one sovereign, the Holy Roman Emperor. It is not the same historical realm as the much larger Roman Empire of the classical era.) The Přemysl dynasty ruled Bohemia on the German kings' behalf until it fell in 1306 with the assassination of Wenceslas III. In the later years of the dynasty, the Přemysls were responsible for uniting the groups of Bohemia and solidifying the region's conversion to Christianity.

The Přemysl dynasty was succeeded by the Luxembourg dynasty, whose first ruler was John of Luxembourg.

"Good King Wenceslas looked out on the Feast of Stephen
When the snow lay round about, deep and crisp and even."

So begins the popular English Christmas carol from 1853, "Good King Wenceslas." It is still sung today, though probably few carolers— aside from the Czechs—know who he was. Wenceslas I (also spelled Wenceslaus), and also known as Václav the Good (ca. 903–935), was Duke of Bohemia in the early Přemysl dynasty. During his rule, Wenceslas promoted Christianity, which had been introduced to Bohemia only a few decades earlier, and was still competing with earlier Slavic religions. He also formed alliances with the rest of Christian Europe, particularly Germany, and extended his dominion in Bohemia.

Czechs consider him the founder of the Czech state. He was an educated man and legends stress his Christian values. His submission to German king Henry I, the Fowler, may be the reason behind his brother Boleslav's conspiracy to murder him in 935. After assassinating his brother, Boleslav (also known as Boleslaus or Boleslaw the Cruel) reigned as duke of Bohemia.

Though the murder of Wenceslas was probably political in nature, it was viewed as martyrdom by the Christian church, and by the beginning of the eleventh century, Wenceslas had attained sainthood. Holy Roman Emperor Otto I (reigned 962–972) posthumously conferred upon him the status of king, which is why, in the legend and the song, he is referred to as the "Good King." Today Saint Wenceslas is the patron saint of Bohemia, and of all the Czech Republic.

(A different Wenceslas I of Bohemia reigned as king of Bohemia from 1230 to 1253. He led a great defense of his homeland against invading Mongols and accomplished much for the development of the Czech state. However, he was not sainted nor did he get his own Christmas carol. Adding to the confusion, there was also Wenceslaus I of Bohemia, duke of Luxembourg, who lived from 1337 to 1383.)

Czech legend proclaims that Saint Wenceslas lies sleeping, along with other Czech knights, under Blaník Mountain in Bohemia. One day, it is said, they will rise under his leadership and return to rid the nation of its enemies.

BOHEMIA'S GOLDEN AGE

Saint Vitus Cathedral in Prague

Bohemia's golden age occurred under the eldest son of John of Luxembourg, also named Wenceslas. He changed his name to Charles and ruled from 1346 to 1378. In 1355 Charles was crowned emperor in Rome, and Prague was chosen as capital of the Holy Roman Empire. As a result, Prague grew to become one of Europe's most important cities politically and culturally, attracting French, Italian, and German scholars, architects, scientists, and artists.

During Charles VI's reign, several of Prague's most significant Gothic buildings were constructed, including Saint Vitus Cathedral and Charles University. The stone Charles Bridge, which he ordered built, is still the main link today between the east and west banks of the capital.

Charles had a great gift for diplomacy, and during his reign there was harmony between the church, the throne, and the nobility. His son, Wenceslas IV, lacked his father's conciliatory skill. During his rule, a reform movement grew, led by Jan Hus, the rector at Bethlehem Chapel. The chapel is significant for another reason—its services were conducted exclusively in Czech rather than Latin.

THE HAPSBURG DYNASTY

The Hapsburgs (also spelled Habsburg), a German royal family whose name derives from the Hapsburg Castle in Switzerland, provided rulers for the Holy Roman Empire, Austria, and Spain. In 1526 Ferdinand I of Hapsburg took up the Czech throne, thus promoting the Hapsburg rule over the country that lasted until 1918. During his reign, he would fight the expansion of the Ottoman Empire into Central Europe. Also during his time, the Protestant Reformation movement broke the Christian Church into two opposing branches, Catholic and Protestant, which caused great upheaval throughout Europe. Ferdinand at first accepted a degree of religious tolerance in Bohemia, where many people had become Lutherans or Hussites.

HUSSITE REFORM MOVEMENT

The Hussite Movement was a pre-Protestant Christian group that began in the Kingdom of Bohemia. Devotees followed the teachings of the Czech priest Jan Hus (YAN HOOS) (c. 1369–1415). Hus studied liberal arts (a group of seven disciplines in medieval universities) and divinity at Charles University, became a professor, and was appointed rector of the university in 1403. In 1400 he was ordained as a priest, and served at Bethlehem Chapel, where he led a movement against corruption in the church.

Jan Hus preaches in this illumination from a 1490 Czech manuscript.

Hus demanded a return to early Christian doctrines and practices, such as the celebration of communion with both bread and wine. He also wanted to rid it of dishonest practices, including charging money for indulgences (the forgiveness of sins) and other religious sacraments.

The university did not support the outspoken Hus, and the archbishop of Prague and Pope John XXIII strongly refuted his doctrines. He was summoned to the Council of Constance in Baden, Germany—the seat of the bishop of the region—to recant the views he was alleged to hold. Jan Hus refused, and after being condemned for heresy, he was burned at the stake on July 6, 1415. (In 1999, Pope John Paul II apologized on behalf of the Catholic Church. He expressed "deep regret for the cruel death inflicted" on Hus and praised his "moral courage.")

Hus's execution ignited two decades of religious and civil war. Bohemia became strongly anti-Catholic during those Hussite Wars, and even after the fighting stopped, the dominion remained independent of the Holy Roman Empire for another two centuries.

The Hussite Movement is sometimes called the Bohemian Reformation. It pre-dated and strongly influenced the Protestant Reformation which spread throughout Europe more than a century later.

This portrait of Ferdinand I, Holy Roman emperor (1558-1564) was painted by the Renaissance artist Hans Bocksberger the Elder.

But over time, the fraught political and religious conflicts in Europe pushed him to establish Catholicism in his realm. The seat of power was moved to Vienna, and Prague became less significant for the Hapsburgs. Rudolf II, Holy Roman Emperor, was crowned the Czech king in 1576, and he moved his court back to Prague in 1583. This move reestablished Prague as the seat of the empire once again.

The Hapsburgs, however, failed to fulfill their promise of religious tolerance. Indignant over that, but perhaps even more so over the loss of traditional privileges, the Protestant Czech upper classes provoked what came to be known as the Thirty Years' War (1618—1648) throughout Central Europe. The Holy Roman Emperor at this time, Ferdinand II (r. 1619—1637), was an even more zealous Catholic than his predecessors, and far less tolerant, which exacerbated the conflict. The war left Bohemia's economy in ruins and spread destruction across much of Central Europe.

The Protestant Czechs were defeated at the Battle of the White Mountain in 1620. The battle consolidated Hapsburg rule and stripped the Czechs of their independence, individual rights and property, and religious freedom. The Protestants were forced to become Catholics. When the Hapsburgs moved the capital back to Vienna, Prague was reduced, culturally and economically, to a sluggish provincial town for more than a century.

THE CZECH NATIONAL REVIVAL MOVEMENT

Nationalist sentiments swept through much of Europe during the late eighteenth and early nineteenth centuries. With more Czechs educated— thanks to the educational reforms instituted by the Hapsburg empress Maria Theresa—a vocal, better informed middle class emerged. Economic reforms forced native Czech laborers into bigger towns, diminishing the influence of the German minorities there.

The revival movement in Prague found expression in literature, theater, and journalism. The leaders of the movement were not political figures but historians and linguists, and the key issues at first were the rights of Czechs to speak and develop a literature in their own language. Although they had been defeated, Czechs continued to push for political independence and the right to use their own language.

THE FIRST REPUBLIC

Many Czechs and Slovaks fought against the Germans and Austrians during World War I. On October 28, 1918, an independent Czechoslovak republic, called the First Republic, was proclaimed with the support of the Allied nations. Prague was designated its capital city and Tomáš Garrigue Masaryk its first president. It was ruled by a coalition of Czech and Slovak parties, and its charter guaranteed equal rights to all citizens. During the first two years of the First Republic, issues about the borders separating the republic from Austria, Germany, and Poland were resolved. Today, Czechs proudly refer to the First Republic as the only liberal democracy at that time in Central Europe.

Tomáš Garrigue Masaryk, the first president of the Republic of Czechoslovakia

THE DARK DAYS OF WORLD WAR II

By the 1930s, three million German speakers lived in Bohemia and most were sympathetic to Adolf Hitler's twisted vision of a grander Germany. The British and French governments pressured Czechoslovakia into giving up Sudetenland, the northwest region of Bohemia adjoining Germany. They believed that such sacrifice would appease Hitler and avoid a war. Opposing the move, President Edvard Beneš of Czechoslovakia resigned on October 5, 1938, and went into exile, first in London, then in Chicago.

As history demonstrates, Hitler was not appeased. On March 14, 1939, Slovakia was also annexed. The next day the Germans occupied Bohemia and Moravia, which the Nazis named the Protectorate of Bohemia and Moravia of the Third Reich. In the period of Nazi repression that followed, Jews were targeted for annihilation, but other Czechs did not escape persecution.

In May 1942, after the assassination of Reinhard Heydrich, a high-ranking Nazi official, by unknown attackers, the Gestapo (abbreviation of Geheime Staatspolizei, German for "Secret State Police") shot to death all the male inhabitants of the mining village of Lidice, accusing them of sheltering the assassins. The women were sent to concentration camps, and the surviving children were parceled out to German families.

As a result of talks between the exiles, including Edvard Beneš and the Soviet Union, the Red Army had great influence on the Czechoslovakian underground movement against the Germans. On May 5, 1945, the people rose up against the German occupiers, and by May 8, after fierce fighting, most of Prague had been liberated. US forces arrived first but allowed the Soviet army to enter Prague as its liberator on May 9.

POSTWAR COMMUNISM

Edvard Beneš returned to Czechoslovakia as president in 1945. In the 1946 election, the Communist Party was the dominant party in the coalition group that formed the government, with Klement Gottwald as prime minister. Tensions soon developed between communist and noncommunist cabinet members.

In January 1948, the Communist Party took over the government by force, with the military backing of the Soviet Union. A new constitution was devised in May, giving the Communist Party total control. President Beneš resigned rather than sanction it, and Gottwald was elected president by the Federal Assembly in June 1948. Industry and agriculture were soon nationalized. Thousands of people fled the country, and many leading figures in Czechoslovak society were imprisoned, executed, or died in labor camps.

The 1950s was an era of harsh political repression and economic decline. During this decade, Czechoslovakia became part of the Warsaw Pact. It was a "treaty of friendship, cooperation, and mutual assistance" between the Soviet Union, Albania, Bulgaria, Czechoslovakia, East Germany, Hungary, Poland, and Romania. It was created as a mutual defense alliance against the forces of the United States, Canada, and Western Europe—which themselves had formed its counterpart, the North Atlantic Treaty Organization (NATO).

However, the Warsaw Pact also provided a way for the Soviet Union to maintain military control over Central and Eastern Europe, as it would demonstrate in the 1968 invasion of Czechoslovakia. The Pact lasted until 1991.

PRAGUE SPRING

Civil liberties increased and censorship practices were loosened during the 1960s, especially toward the end of that decade under the new president, Alexander Dubček. That period of restored freedoms is known as the "Prague Spring." Soviet-bloc leaders became very agitated by the Czech moves toward a realized democracy, and on August 21, 1968, Warsaw Pact troops and tanks invaded the country.

In the following decade, thousands of Communist Party members were expelled from the party and lost their jobs. Many professionals and other educated civilians were forced to earn their living doing menial jobs. That was followed in the 1980s by economic and political stagnation, corruption of the state system, and severely lowered living standards. Prior to

Czech children play on a burnt-out Soviet tank in August 1968, following the events of the Prague Spring.

World War II, Czechoslovakia had enjoyed the tenth-highest standard of living in the world. By the end of the 1980s, it had plunged to 42nd place, well below many developing nations. This contributed to a growing dissatisfaction with the communist regime.

THE VELVET REVOLUTION

In 1977 the country's intellectuals signed a petition known as Charter 77, listing their grievances against the repressive communist regime. It failed in producing changes, but in the decade that followed, members of that group played an important role in fomenting dissatisfaction against the regime. Toward the end of 1989, the citizens of Czechoslovakia began expressing strong discontent with the communist regime.

The first of several demonstrations took place on August 21, 1989, the twenty-first anniversary of the crushing of the Prague Spring. The demonstrators—a mix of young and old, intellectuals and laborers—sang the national anthem and waved the national flag as they demanded freedom of expression, thought, association, and belief. Censorship had controlled all aspects of their lives. They wanted the freedom to decide what music to play and what books to read without fear of government reprisal.

On November 17, 1989, the anniversary of the death of nine students killed by the Nazis in 1939, Prague's communist youth organized an officially sanctioned demonstration in Wenceslas Square in Prague. That venerated square, the symbolic heart of the country, is presided over by the statue of Wenceslas, the country's patron saint.

The students declared an indefinite strike and were joined by actors and musicians. Although it was a peaceful protest, riot police were sent in to suppress the students. As a result, a week of demonstrations followed in Prague in which, in a city of two million, more than 750,000 people participated. On November 27, ten days after the student strike, a general strike was held; over half the population stopped working for two hours.

The strike precipitated the resignation of the communist chairperson of the Federal Assembly and heralded the collapse of the communist government. On December 28, 1989, the dissident playwright Václav Havel was elected president, Václav Klaus was elected prime minister, and Alexander Dubček became the speaker of parliament. The days that followed came to be called the "Velvet Revolution" because there were no casualties.

Following the overthrow of communism, the Havel government had two main objectives: to ensure the first free elections since 1946 and to make a rapid push toward a free-market economy. That process involved the return of property to its original owners (pre-1948) and the privatization of most state-owned industry.

Czechs in general were more in favor of radical economic reform than the Slovaks, because the Slovaks were suffering greater economic hardship and higher unemployment from a declining arms industry. Another deep-rooted issue was the resentment the Slovaks felt at having been treated as second-class citizens for many decades. Those sentiments were fueled by the election of the Movement for a Democratic Slovakia party in June 1992 in Slovakia. The party leader, Vladimír Mečiar, was a strong supporter of complete independence for Slovaks and slower economic reform. The Civic Democratic Party won the election in the Czech lands. During postelection negotiations between the two parties, Václav Klaus, leader of the Civic Democratic Party, insisted on separation.

THE VELVET DIVORCE

President Václav Havel resigned in protest, refusing to preside over the split. In the first few months of independence, relations between the two republics were determined by twenty-five interstate treaties that provided a framework for issues such as the division of property, federal institutions, and a common currency. Prague became the capital of the Czech Republic, Václav Havel was once again elected the president, and Václav Klaus became prime minister.

AFTER INDEPENDENCE

The Czech Republic became a member of NATO on March 12, 1999, and joined the European Union (EU) on May 1, 2004. Both events are significant

Extraordinary times tend to produce extraordinary people—or is it the other way around? For the Czech populace, Václav Havel (VA-tslaf HAH-vel) (1936–2011) was just such a person. He was the last president of Czechoslovakia and the first president of the Czech Republic following the Velvet Divorce. But he was more than just another politician, and when he died in December 2011, The New York Times *said, "Mr. Havel came to personify the soul of the Czech nation."*

Before he became a national leader, he was a well-known writer, poet, and playwright, and a thorn in the side of his country's communist government. Not by coincidence, his early plays were absurdist indictments of communism and the dehumanizing aspects of bureaucracy. An active participant in the Prague Spring demonstrations, he later found his plays banned and his passport confiscated. Uncowed, he continued to work and write as a dissident despite frequent arrests and a four-year stint in prison. His famous 1978 essay, "The Power of the Powerless," officially banned at the time, helped to galvanize the Czech opposition. He played a major role in the Velvet Revolution that finally ousted communism, and when a new democratic government was formed, he was popularly elected president.

During his time as president, Havel turned his nation's sights toward the West. He worked to dismantle the Warsaw Pact and in its place, paved the way for the Czech Republic to join NATO and the European Union. Although he had his critics at home, he enjoyed tremendous acclaim worldwide for his eloquent defense of freedom and human rights. After his death, US President Barack Obama said, "His peaceful resistance shook the foundations of an empire, exposed the emptiness of a repressive ideology, and proved that moral leadership is more powerful than any weapon."

landmarks in the nation's history. The country is also a member of the United Nations and the World Trade Organization.

Although the Czech Republic has achieved a great deal since its independence, the government still faces important challenges in many areas, including completing its economic restructuring, eliminating corruption, improving its environmental performance, and reforming its failed health service as well as retooling its pensions program.

In December 2011, former President Václav Havel died at age seventy-five, and the country observed a week of mourning. In 2012, the international airport in Prague was renamed in his honor.

In July 2016, the Czech Republic adopted the informal name Czechia as an alternative short form in English. The Czech Republic remains its official formal name. In the Czech language, those names are Česká republika and Česko. Therefore, Czechia is seen as the English translation of Česko.

INTERNET LINKS

http://www.bbc.com/news/world-europe-17220571
The BBC News provides a timeline of key events in the Czech Republic, but it does not include the earlier history of the region.

http://www.czech.cz/en/Home-en
Among its other features, this official Czech website offers articles about Czech history.

http://www.localhistories.org/czech.html
This site has no pictures, but provides a basic history of the land from ancient times to the present.

http://www.nytimes.com/2011/12/19/world/europe/vaclav-havel-dissident-playwright-who-led-czechoslovakia-dead-at-75.html
The New York Times obituary for Václav Havel paints an eloquent portrait of the iconic Czech leader.

GOVERNMENT

A guard stands on duty at Prague Castle.

3

THE CZECH REPUBLIC IS A parliamentary republic with a president, a prime minister, and a bicameral (two-house) parliament. It is a multi-party democracy with universal suffrage at age eighteen. The capital is Prague and the country consists of fourteen administrative districts—thirteen regions plus the capital city.

A man casts his vote during the 2017 elections.

"I dream of a republic independent, free, and democratic, of a republic economically prosperous and yet socially just. ... Of a republic of well-rounded people, because without such people it is impossible to solve any of our problems—human, economic, ecological, social, or political."
—President Václav Havel, New Year's Address to the Nation, 1990.

THE PREAMBLE OF THE CONSTITUTION

"We, the citizens of the Czech Republic in Bohemia, Moravia, and Silesia, at this time of the reconstitution of an independent Czech State, true to all the sound traditions of the ancient statehood of the Lands of the Czech Crown as well as of Czechoslovak statehood, resolve to build, protect, and advance the Czech Republic in the spirit of the inalienable values of human dignity and freedom as the home of equal and free citizens who are aware of their obligations toward others and of their responsibility to the community."

THE CONSTITUTION

The structure of the government and its laws are based on the Constitution. The one in use today dates to the founding of the country in 1993. It has been amended eight times, most recently in 2013. In 2011, an amendment changed the way the president is elected, now providing for election by popular vote. Prior to that, the president had been elected by a joint session of the parliament. The 2013 amendment allows for citizens to have dual nationalities.

Many of the constitution's Western liberal principles are similar to those of the constitution for the noncommunist, post-1989 federation of Czechoslovakia, which was written in a very difficult period, amid tension and differences of opinion between Czech and Slovakian leaders. The Czechs have enshrined in their constitution their solemn desire for democracy and freedom, as well as their recognition of their responsibilities as individual citizens and as a community.

THE EXECUTIVES

The president is the head of state and is elected for a term of five years. The prime minister and the cabinet (the board of ministers), though, wield the greater power. The prime minister is head of government and is chosen by the president and approved by the parliament. He or she is the head of the cabinet and advises the president on the selection of the other cabinet

members. The cabinet consists of the prime minister, deputy prime ministers, and ministers.

The first president of the Czech Republic, Václav Havel, elected in 1993, presided over his country at a time of momentous change—the fall of communism, the end of a seventy-four-year-old state, and the creation of two separate republics, as well as the transformation of his country from a socialist state to a free-market, democratic state.

Václav Klaus was the first prime minister of the Czech Republic in 1993. He was also the leader of the Civic Democratic Party, the dominant party in the coalition formed after the June 1992 elections. In the same elections, Vladimír Mečiar, the leader of the Movement for Democratic Slovakia, became the Slovakian prime minister. The Czechoslovak federation ended after these elections.

Klaus went on to become president in 2003 and served a second term from 2008 to 2012. In 2013, Milos Zeman (b. 1944) became president under the new absolute majority popular vote system brought about by the constitutional amendment of that same year. He will be eligible for reelection in 2018. Zeman previously served as prime minister from 1998 to 2002. The

Visitors come and go at the entrance to the Old Royal Palace in Prague.

president serves for five years and can serve a maximum of two consecutive terms, which Zeman hopes to serve. In 2017, he announced his candidacy for reelection. In December 2017, Andrej Babiš (b. 1954) became prime minister, a four-year position.

The Czech cabinet is appointed by the president on the recommendation of the prime minister. Apart from the prime minister, the government currently has seventeen members heading the following departments: Transport; Finance; Culture; Defense; Labor and Social Affairs; Regional Development; Industry and Trade; Justice; Education, Youth and Sport; Interior; Foreign Affairs; Health; Agriculture, Environment, Science and Research, and Human Rights and Equal Opportunities.

THE HOUSES OF PARLIAMENT

The parliament is made up of two chambers, or houses: the senate (upper house) and the chamber of deputies (lower house). Representatives in both are elected by popular vote according to proportional representation. The chamber of deputies consists of two hundred deputies, each of whom is

Straka Academy, the seat of the Czech government in Prague, originally served as a boarding school for impoverished descendants of Czech noble families. During World War I, it was a Red Cross hospital.

He is a billionaire businessman turned politician that some political observers have likened to Donald Trump. Andrej Babiš is the second-richest man in the Czech Republic and a scandal-ridden public figure. He ran for president on an anti-immigrant populist campaign pledging to run the country like a business. He also has close ties with Russian President Vladimir Putin.

In 2011, he founded the ANO (Action for Dissatisfied Citizens) political party as a protest alternative to the established parties. From 2014 to May 2017, he served as first deputy prime minister and the minister of finance under the outgoing Prime Minister Bohuslav Sobotka (b. 1971). Charging Babiš with financial misconduct, Sobotka fired the minister. Babiš had allegedly avoided paying taxes during his time as CEO of Agrofert, the third-largest company in the Czech Republic and a conglomerate of more than 230 companies that he himself founded. During his tenure as finance minister, he is said to have passed laws benefitting large corporations like his own at the expense of smaller businesses.

In October 2017, the same month he won the presidential election by a landslide, Babiš was formally charged with tax fraud and old cases were reopened of his suspected cooperation with communist-era secret police. Regardless of these allegations, he has been very popular with the public, which has become disenchanted with established politicians because of corruption or unfulfilled promises.

elected for a term of four years. Czech citizens aged twenty-one and older are eligible to be elected to the chamber of deputies.

The senate has eighty senators who serve six-year terms. Czech citizens forty years of age and older may be elected to the senate.

JUDICIARY

The judicial system includes the Supreme Court (organized into civil, commercial, and criminal divisions); the Constitutional Court; and the Supreme Administrative Court. The president appoints the judges of the Supreme and Constitutional courts, and the senate approves or rejects the nominations. Supreme Court justices are appointed for life; Constitutional court judges serve for ten-year renewable terms. Supreme Administrative Court judges selected by the president of the Court serve for unlimited terms.

There are civil, criminal, commercial, and administrative courts. When disputes are related to business, the people concerned go to a commercial court to settle matters. Administrative courts are courts of appeal for citizens who question the legality of decisions made in state institutions.

The courts under the Ministry of Justice have a clear hierarchy: they are at republic, regional, and district levels. The first point of appeal is the district court, where cases are usually decided by a panel consisting of a judge and two associate judges. Associate judges are citizens of good standing over the age of twenty-four, elected for four years. The regional courts deal with more serious cases and also may act as courts of appeal for district courts. In both district and regional courts, a single judge rather than a panel of judges will occasionally decide these cases.

Military courts are convened under the jurisdiction of the Ministry of Defense. The Supreme Court interprets the law, acts as a guide to other courts, and also functions as a court of appeal.

MILITARY

The Czech armed forces include the army and air forces. Because the nation is landlocked, there is no navy. Compulsory military service was abolished at the close of 2004, ending 140 years of military obligation for Czech men.

Under the communist regime, military strength was approximately two hundred thousand personnel on active duty. The Czech Republic has reduced the number of its military personnel to approximately thirty thousand, with about 22,000 on active duty and seven thousand on reserve. Besides the army and air force, there are also civil defense, railroad, and internal security units. The president of the republic is the military commander-in-chief.

The Czech Republic flag.

THE FLAG

The traditional flag of the Czech lands had two equal horizontal bands of white and red. Because this is identical to the flags of other former Soviet bloc countries, the Czech Republic chose to use the flag of Czechoslovakia, which combines the white and red colors of Bohemia with a triangle of the blue in the Moravian coat of arms. This choice raised a storm of controversy with Slovakia, for the two republics had already agreed not to use the old federal symbols.

INTERNET LINKS

https://www.cia.gov/library/publications/the-world-factbook /geos/ez.html
The CIA World Factbook has information on the Czech government.

https://www.constituteproject.org/constitution/Czech_ Republic_2013.pdf?lang=en
An English translation of the Czech constitution is posted here.

https://www.vlada.cz
This is the site of the Czech government; which can be translated into English.

ECONOMY

Various denominations of colorful koruna, the bank notes of the Czech Republic

4

A FTER THE COMMUNIST REGIME ended in 1989, changing from a centrally-planned economy to a free-market economy under democracy was a formidable challenge. But the Czech Republic accomplished this and became one of the most stable and successful post-communist countries in all of Europe. In 2004, the Czech Republic joined the European Union (EU), along with Poland, Slovakia, Hungary, Lithuania, Latvia, Estonia, Slovenia, Cyprus, and Malta. The EU is an association of twenty-eight European nations for the purposes of political and economic integration. (In 2016, the United Kingdom voted to withdraw from the EU in 2019.)

The country's low unemployment rate has led to steady increases in salaries in recent years. However, with a shortage of skilled workers, businesses are asking the government to allow greater migration of qualified workers, especially from Ukraine and neighboring Central European countries.

TWO PHASES OF REFORM

While he was prime minister, Václav Klaus instigated a two-phase privatization plan. The first phase required the return of property to pre-1948 owners, or their descendants, and called for the sale of enterprises through auctions or directly to foreign buyers. That phase was quite successful, with almost 16,500 units privatized and 183 units returned to former owners. Today, most restaurants, hotels, and retail stores are privately owned, while the government still owns some theaters, museums, and castles. Many banks that were state-run have been privatized. There are now both local and international banks with branches in the Czech Republic.

The second phase of the plan concentrated on large-scale industries and small enterprises that had not found buyers. A coupon system was introduced to give every citizen a chance to become a shareholder. After January 1994 the coupons could be exchanged for shares in over 770 unsold companies. The idea was accepted enthusiastically by most Czechs and Slovaks at the time, with 8.5 million people buying coupons. This phase also focused on the return of confiscated property to the Catholic Church, the implementation of a bankruptcy law, and the privatization of agriculture and health care.

A PROSPEROUS ECONOMY

Although the Czech Republic weathered a rocky economic path after the Velvet Divorce, the republic has now successfully embraced the new market economy. Today it is one of the most prosperous of the former communist states. The economic growth rate has been as high as 6.5 percent in some years, but slowed to about 2.6 percent in 2016. As of October 2017, the unemployment rate was the lowest in the EU at 2.7 percent and in 2015, the poverty rate was the lowest in Europe.

Czechia's exports comprise some 80 percent of GDP and largely consist of automobiles, the country's largest industry. The country joined the EU in 2004, but has yet to join the euro-zone, meaning it has retained its own currency, the Czech koruna (CZK) rather than adopt the euro.

Since coming to power in 2014, the government has instituted reforms to try to reduce corruption, attract investment, and improve social welfare programs. In 2016, it introduced an online tax reporting system intended to reduce tax evasion—and therefore increase revenues. The government also plans to improve the business climate, bringing certain procedures in line with EU best practices, and to boost wages. The country's low unemployment rate has led to steady increases in salaries. This has led to growing domestic demand among the Czech people for all kinds of products, from automotives to home mortgages. Increased use of credit cards has also contributed to greater demand for goods and services.

The Czech Republic's industrial base includes the production of steel, iron, cement, ceramics, plastics, cotton, clothing, and beer. The timber industry provides most of the wood required for newsprint, furniture, plywood, and traditional woodworking. Of the 5.35 million person labor force, almost 60 percent work in service categories and 38 percent in industry. The number of people employed in agriculture has decreased dramatically.

Czechia's economic future now depends on building a more skilled population of workers, and diversifying away from manufacturing and toward a more high-tech, services-based, knowledge economy.

A train carries new Hyundai cars manufactured in the Czech Republic to Germany.

AGRICULTURE

Crop production has declined since the late 1980s. Under communism, land that had been private property became state property and was exhaustively overcultivated. Communism guaranteed farmers a wage, no matter how much they produced, so they did not have to work efficiently. Since the farm they worked was state owned, they did not have to make it commercially worthwhile. Consequently, a farm machinery breakdown was seen as lucky, as the farmer could not work at all until the equipment was repaired—and repairs often took weeks.

Today, many Czechs cannot claim their old land because it is impossible to determine which section of it was once theirs. Many are reluctant to make a claim, anyway, because to make the land financially viable will require much

A farmer plants potatoes in the springtime.

effort and investment. Ironically, many owners of small plots are joining cooperatives in order to make a living. It will be many years before the land becomes productive once again, and there is still a shortage of appropriate technology on the smaller farms.

In most EU countries, the majority of the agricultural land is owned by the farmers, but in the Czech Republic the farmland is generally rented by the persons who work on it. According to the agricultural census of 2010, only 22 percent of the Czech farmland belonged to the farmers who actually worked it.

Although the country has ample fertile land and resources, it is still not self-sufficient in food production. A basic problem is organization and distribution. Fruit on the trees in the countryside remains unpicked, while grapes imported from Spain are sold in the city streets. It may be simply a question of time before agriculture absorbs the effects of rapid economic change and of the reduced labor force to become a successful sector again.

The major crops are sugar beets, wheat, potatoes, corn, barley, rye, and hops. The preferred livestock are cattle, pigs, chickens, and horses. The dairy industry continues to supply most domestic requirements. South Bohemia has a well-established fish-farm industry, consisting mainly of carp cultivation. Remarkably, these carp lakes were excavated during the Middle Ages. Carp is a traditional dish at Christmas.

RESOURCES AND ENERGY

There are limited reserves of coal, coke, timber, uranium, and iron ore in the Czech Republic. Central Bohemia, between Prague and Plzeň, is an important region for iron ore mining. Lead and zinc ore are mined near Kutná Hora and Příbram in Bohemia, and in the northeast of the country; uranium in Příbram and in the northern regions of Bohemia; and tin in the Ore Mountains to the northeast.

The major centers for coal mining and manufacturing traditionally have been in the northern regions of Bohemia. Severe air pollution, a side effect of burning low-quality brown coal (lignite), is a serious problem there. As the country upgrades to meet EU standards, this should improve.

All of the inhabited parts of the country are wired for electricity. At present, most electricity comes from coal-burning plants and the nuclear reactors at Dukovany. Oil and natural gas are imported from Russia. To reduce fuel dependency on Russia, an oil pipeline through Germany was constructed, and a nuclear power plant opened in 2002 at Temelín. That was a communist project that the post-1989 government decided to complete, modifying the original Soviet design with Western safety technology and procedures. The controversial project has been the focus of protests by antinuclear activists, including some overseas environmentalists. However, the government's commitment to nuclear power is strong. About one-third of the nation's electricity is generated by nuclear power and plans are to increase that capacity significantly.

TRANSPORTATION

Trams and buses run along the streets of Prague.

TRAINS AND BUSES The Czech Republic has an extremely comprehensive railway infrastructure that stretches 75 miles (120 km) of railroads per 386 square miles (1,000 square km) of the country. Czech Railways owns and operates approximately 5,894 miles (9,483 km) of railway lines. Over 180 million passengers and over 110 million tons (100 million metric tonnes) of goods are transported annually by Czech railways.

The state railway company was dissolved after the Velvet Divorce. Today, improvements continue to be made to the network, including the connection of core rails to main European lines, meeting the requirements of EU standards as well as improving safety, speed, and reliability.

Buses and streetcars tend to be cheap and fast. Buses connect the suburbs to city centers; some cover even longer distances. Commuters in Prague have the option of traveling by subway. Commuters purchase train, subway, streetcar, and bus tickets at tobacco stands, newsstands, and ticket-vending machines in the larger cities. Timetables for public transportation can also be purchased at bookstores.

ON THE ROAD The republic has a network of good roads. The Czech highway system, made up of motorways (superhighways) and high-speed roads, is continually being developed and improved. When completed, the total distance will extend to 1,305 miles (2,100 km).Some of the more important motorways include Motorway D1 that connects Prague to Brno; Motorway D5 that connects Prague, Plzeň, and Rozvadov; and Motorway D11 from Prague to Kolín.

An electronic toll system was launched in 2007. This toll applies to all vehicles, except motorcycles, that use motorways, expressways, and certain other roads. All vehicles subject to the toll are required to be equipped with an electronic device that collects the necessary fee from a prepaid account while the vehicle passes through the tollgate.

An increasing number of Czechs own cars, which means that highways and country roads now have heavier traffic than they used to. As in the rest of Europe and the United States, vehicles are driven on the right side of the road. The legal driving age is eighteen. Penalties for speeding and drunk driving are very high. The theft of cars and valuables from cars has become a major problem in the larger cities.

IN THE AIR There are four big international airports: in Prague, Ostrava, Brno, and Karlovy Vary. The Václav Havel Airport Prague (formerly the Prague Ruzyně International Airport) is by far the biggest airport in the Czech Republic. It serves some fifteen million passengers each year and accommodates sixty-six airlines. The airport serves 154 national and international destinations.

BOATS Boat transportation in the Czech Republic makes use of several large rivers: the Elbe (the Labe), the Vltava (the lower reaches), and the Berounka. Among other rivers that can be used are some stretches of the Morava, Bečva, and Odra. Boats are used mainly for transporting freight throughout the country. Traveling by boat is popular in Prague among visitors, as the many waterways promise interesting sightseeing.

INTERNET LINKS

http://www.czech.cz/en/Business/Economic-facts/Development-of -Czech-economy
This site provides provides a quick synopsis of the Czech economy.

https://europa.eu/european-union/about-eu/countries/member -countries/czechrepublic_en
The EU site gives an overview of its member nation, the Czech Republic.

ENVIRONMENT

PŘÍRODNÍ REZERVACE

The Czech Republic national emblem adorns a sign in the snowy woods, indicating that this is a protected nature reserve.

5

LIKE OTHER FORMER COMMUNIST countries in Eastern Europe, the Czech Republic is still struggling to clean up the damage caused by decades of disregard for the environment. Parts of the republic are among the most polluted areas in the world. The concentration of light industry in northern Bohemia and Moravia since the industrial revolution has been exacerbated by the introduction of heavy industry during the communist years. The burning of low-grade brown coal is primarily responsible for sulfur emissions and other pollutants that contribute to acid rain. This acidic precipitation is harmful to plant life; in the Czech Republic, it has affected 60 percent of the forests in the country, and polluted waterways as well.

Prague is the site of some of the worst air pollution in the country. In the winter, when people are using their home furnaces and power plants are running at peak production, pollution often reaches dangerous levels.

The Czech Republic's commitment to focus more on the environment became evident in 1990 when the Ministry of the Environment of the Czech Republic was established.

According to a 2017 Environment Ministry report, between six thousand and eight thousand Czechs die each year of air pollution-related diseases. In heavily affected areas such as the Ostrava region, air pollution contributes to the early death of as many as 10 percent of the people who die there.

FORESTS

Forests make up a significant part of the Czech Republic's physical environment, covering about 34.4 percent of the country. In the 1980s, acid rain destroyed as many as one-third of forest trees, particularly in the northern part of the nation. Consequently, the rate of defoliation, or leaf loss, in the Czech Republic was once one of the highest in Europe. The forests of the Jizera Mountains were particularly hard hit.

However, the total area of the country's forest land has been constantly growing, thanks in large part to replanting, better forest management, and the shift to greener technologies. This increase is evidence that most Czech forests are thriving. Even so, pollution levels must be continuously monitored and controlled to ensure that the forests remain in a healthy state.

Autumn colors shine in the vibrant sunlight in the České Švýcarsko (Bohemian Switzerland) National Park.

FLOODS

Floods are a natural hazard in the Czech Republic. The decline in its forest areas in the past had no doubt resulted in more severe floods, since tree roots restrain soil erosion. The land has suffered greatly as a result of severe flooding.

In 1997 major flooding affected large parts of Moravia, in particular the area around Ostrava, which is the industrial heartland of the nation. Many people were killed or injured, and massive damage crippled the infrastructure, including roads, mines, foundries, telecommunications, and utilities. Telephone lines and power cables came

In June 2013, the Elbe River floods the city of Ústí nad Labem in Northern Bohemia.

down, and thousands of miles of roads were washed away.

In August 2002 the Czech Republic again was hit by devastating floods in what was the biggest and worst natural disaster in modern Czech history. There were seventeen deaths and thousands of people had to be evacuated from their homes. These floods caused damages of over $2.5 million. Prague was badly affected, particularly in the flooded areas below the castle, in the Jewish quarter, and in other traditional neighborhoods. Authorities ordered over 50,000 residents to evacuate their homes, and residents as well as thousands of tourists were given strict warnings to keep away from danger areas, including parts of the popular historical center.

Again in June 2013, Prague experienced severe flooding and six people died as a result. Some seven thousand people were evacuated and even the tigers at the Prague Zoo were tranquilized and moved to a drier location.

Climate scientists predict that the conditions causing such floods in Central Europe will become more frequent as a result of climate change.

The forests have a long list of useful functions, including acting as pollution filters and soil protectors, as well as helping to stabilize the climate. The Czech economy also relies on its abundant forests as the source of valuable timber it exports to other countries. In parts of the country, however, irresponsible felling practices and poor management have impacted the forests negatively, and their corresponding ecosystems have suffered, too. The results of a Czech government research study promoted the following methods of improving forest soils—planting of deciduous trees, elimination of clear-cutting practices, and retention of dead and decaying wood in the forests. The implementation of these recommendations is expected to ensure that the forests continue to thrive.

An unusual source of forest damage is caused by the large numbers of European and roe deer that forage in some Czech forests. Although these graceful animals are hunted for food, their huge numbers make them unsustainable. The droves of deer also damage delicate tree saplings. Another harmful impact to the precious forests lies in the continued attempts by business and government alike to profit from the trees without concern for their natural functions.

NATIONAL PARKS

In spite of the many problems caused by assaults on the forests, there still remain several beautiful national parks and forest areas in the Czech Republic. In order to preserve these areas of outstanding natural beauty, a small number of national parks and forests are under careful supervision. These include the primeval forests of Boubín, Mionší, Bílá Opava, Ranšpurk, Žofín, and Trojmezí. A few others are regarded as jewels of Czech nature and important subjects of scientific research. Conserving these beautiful areas is essential to maintain the biodiversity of the region. There are four national parks—Krkonoše, Šumava, Podyjí, and České Švýcarsko. In addition, there are twenty-five regions that have been established as Protected Landscape Areas.

Šumava National Park is located in the Plzeň and South Bohemian regions of the Czech Republic along the border with Germany and Austria. The Šumava Range is made up of the most extensive forest in Central Europe. It is covered mainly with spruce trees. It is possible to see lynx in this beautiful area.

Krkonoše National Park is a UNESCO Biosphere Reserve site. It is located in the Liberec and Hradec Králové regions and lies in the Czech Republic's highest mountain range, the Krkonoše Mountains.

Podyjí National Park is located in the South Moravian region. This unique park is home to primeval forests.

The České Švýcarsko National Park was established in January 2000 and shares a border with Germany.

Trees tower in the Podyji National Park in Moravia.

FLORA AND FAUNA

Almost 70 percent of the Czech forest is home to mixed or deciduous flora and a large variety of fauna. Some original steppe grassland areas are still found in the region of Moravia, but today most of these lowlands have been cultivated.

Mammals that are commonly found in the Czech Republic include the fox, hare, deer, rabbit, and wild pig. A variety of birds inhabit the Czech lowlands and valleys. Fish such as carp, pike, and trout are found in most rivers and natural and man-made ponds.

Many important improvements have been made to the environment in recent years. As a result, some species of plants and animals are starting to reappear after many years' absence in nature, ranging from mushrooms and lichens to vertebrates. The Czech Republic belongs to the NATURA 2000 network that aims to maintain and restore the populations of species and their natural habitats.

Wild pigs roam the forests of the Czech Republic, where they are hunted for their meat.

ENDANGERED SPECIES

In spite of the many positive changes being made to the Czech environment, sadly, some types of animals and plants are disappearing from the country altogether. There are many reasons for this, some of them unknown. Many believe, however, that one of the main causes may be the deliberate destruction inflicted by humans.

The endangered list, compiled by the International Union for Conservation of Nature (IUCN), includes seven mammal species, six bird species, six types of freshwater fish, and seven plant species.

Endangered species include the Atlantic sturgeon, slender-billed curlew, and Spengler's freshwater mussel. Other vulnerable animals include the Bechstein's bat, Eurasian otter, European squirrel, garden dormouse, Geoffroy's bat, lesser horseshoe bat, pond bat, and the Western barbastelle bat.

ECOTOURISM

Like many other countries that fortunately have areas of outstanding natural beauty, the Czech Republic has started to promote its green, or ecotourism, programs. These invite the visitor to enjoy local nature, forests, and wildlife flora and fauna. Moreover, ecotourism ensures that the detrimental aspects of conventional tourism on the Czech environment are minimized. Popular ecotours include cycling, hiking, and bird-watching.

WATER

The long-term annual average precipitation in the Czech Republic is equal to about 26 inches (672 millimeters). More than half of the nation's fresh water is used for industry and only 1 percent is used for farming. Czechs in urban and rural areas everywhere have access to safe drinking water.

The main Czech rivers, including the Elbe, Vltava, Morava, Dyje, and Oder, have maintained good water quality. Nevertheless, certain rivers, such as the Jihlava, Lužnice, and Bílina, carry extremely polluted water, though improvements are being made to make the water safer for swimming and water sports.

POLLUTION

The Czech Republic suffers from a poor history of pollution, with air, water, and land pollution among the highest in the EU. This has been caused mainly by industry, mining, and agriculture. In some parts of the country where pollution levels are excessive, there is a high percentage of residents who have become afflicted with lung cancer and other diseases caused by their contaminated surroundings.

AIR POLLUTION Parts of the Czech Republic are among the most polluted in the world. The concentration of light industry in northern Bohemia and Moravia since the industrial revolution has been exacerbated by the introduction of heavy industry during the communist years. The

A steel factory in Ostrava emits pollution into the air.

contamination of the republic's air is a result of the widespread use of lignite as a source of energy during the communist era. The levels of sulfur dioxide that were emitted were some of the highest in the whole of Europe. The burning of the low-grade brown coal is primarily responsible for the high quantities of sulfur that industry emits annually. The situation so concerned the other Western European countries that they offered financial help to encourage Czechs to try to reduce their migrating pollution. Large strides were made in the 1990s to improve their air pollution profile.

Prague is the site of some of the worst air pollution in the country. In the winter, when more energy is expended to provide heating for people, the pollution can shoot up to very dangerous levels.

These dangerous levels of air pollution can lead to respiratory illnesses that may ultimately lead to death. In the past, public attention tended to be more focused on creating a better standard of living than on the environment. To meet European criteria, in 2004 the senate passed a law on improving air quality, and the government is working hard to cut emission levels from over a hundred major polluters.

Air pollution in the Czech Republic has improved during the last decade as a result of a decreasing consumption of brown coal, with its high content of sulfur dioxide, used in large power plants. As in other parts of Europe, Czech air pollution is also made worse by toxic traffic emissions.

While the Czech Republic enjoys cleaner air and reduced levels of smog today, some regions still suffer from poor air conditions. In other regions, it should be noted that the air quality is better than in some other EU countries.

WATER POLLUTION Between 1993 and 2010, there was a significant decrease in the amount of pollution discharged into the waterways in the Czech Republic. As a result of the modernization and construction of several hundred new wastewater treatment plants in larger cities and towns, the quality of water has improved tremendously. The country now has 2,100 water treatment plants, but still needs to update water treatment in some smaller municipalities.

With underground water reserves declining dramatically, the Ministry of Environment has been working on new measures to fight drought.

A sewage treatment plant in Pilsen cleans water for recycling.

LAND EROSION The decrease in mining of brown and black coal has put a stop to the devastation of the natural landscape of the North Bohemian and Sokolov brown coal-mining areas. Similarly, a reduction in uranium mining has gradually improved conditions in western Bohemia. The Czech Republic also suffers from significant land erosion brought about by poor agricultural and mining practices.

NOISE POLLUTION The number of vehicles using Czech roads is increasing rapidly. This growth inevitably leads to a rise in the noise and air pollution levels. The shift from using public transportation—trains, streetcars, and buses—to using cars will undoubtedly generate negative consequences for the environment, especially increased air pollution.

Although all types of pollution continue to be an obstinate problem in the Czech Republic, the people and the government together are working hard to rectify the situation. In fact, many improvements have been made in recent years.

THE MODERN CZECH LANDSCAPE

In the 1990s, the Czech Republic experienced many changes at a rapid pace. As a result, little time was given to the proper planning, for example, of new buildings. Czech towns and cities today are usually blighted by buildings of a poor quality. The sudden building boom, brought about partly by the changes to the economy, has inadvertently but adversely affected the Czech rural and urban environment.

An abandoned factory in Ostrava falls in disrepair and ruin.

A positive change is that in many cities, large towns, and municipalities today, there is a noticeable improvement in the cleanliness of public areas and streets. Nonetheless, there still exist numerous unlicensed dumps, and unsightly litter is seen in many areas of larger cities.

Many Czech cities and towns are becoming more built-up and cramped with new buildings and defiled by advertising billboards. The areas at the edges of many towns and cities, which used to be farmland, are now being used as industrial and commercial zones. Unfortunately, there are also many unoccupied buildings that are slowly deteriorating and other properties that simply have been abandoned.

WASTE MANAGEMENT

Joining the EU motivated the Czech Republic to clean up and improve its waste management practices. Nevertheless, illegal waste dumps are still eyesores on the landscape. Recycling, once an uncommon practice in Czech households, is catching on as people become accustomed to the new, stricter rules required by the EU. These EU mandates require that 50 percent of all waste be recycled by 2020 and 65 percent by 2030.

In order to meet that requirement, the Czech government has implemented a landfill tax. Now, about 70 percent of municipal solid waste in the country is landfill. After 2024, however, landfilling recyclable waste will be prohibited as the country switches to waste incineration and waste-to-energy plants.

THE FUTURE

The dramatic political changes that have occurred in the Czech Republic since independence have generally had a favorable impact on the environment.

Many of the republic's younger generation show an eagerness to learn about all environmental matters and are ready to make the necessary improvements for the good of their new country.

During the years following the fall of communism and the breakup of Czechoslovakia, Czech businesses and the new Czech government tended to focus on creating a strong economy. They had little time or interest for environmental issues. Today, however, as the economy has become more stable and successful, more is being done to tackle environmental issues. There are even incentives in place to encourage good environmental practices in business and industry.

INTERNET LINKS

https://www.eea.europa.eu/soer-2015/countries/czech-republic
The European Environment Agency report on the Czech Republic includes a map of air quality.

http://www.mzp.cz/en
The Ministry of the Environment of the Czech Republic site provides information on a variety of related topics.

http://www.mzp.cz/C125750E003B698B/en/czech_republic_strategy_sd/$FILE/KM-SFSD_CR_EN-20100317.pdf
The Strategic Framework for Sustainable Development in the Czech Republic lays out the country's objectives for "green" economic growth.

CZECHS

A man in traditional folk clothing leads a horse carrying the king's courtiers during the Ride of the Kings festival in May 2017.

6

THE CZECH REPUBLIC, BEING NAMED after the people who live in it— rather than the other way around— has a largely homogenous population numbering some 10,674,700 people. By far, the dominant group is made up of ethnic Czechs, part of a West Slavic ethnic group common to Central Europe. Those peoples trace their lineage back to tribes who occupied the region in the ninth and tenth centuries—particularly the Bohemians and Moravians. They, in turn, were the descendants of Slavonic groups that migrated into Central Europe during the fifth and sixth centuries CE. Those groups inhabited the regions of Bohemia and Moravia as well as western Slovakia, eastern Germany, southern Poland (including Silesia), and northern Hungary.

The Czech national identity is founded on a folk legend. In mythical times (probably sometime in the sixth or seventh century), Forefather Czech (or Čech) led his people on a journey in search of a new homeland. After climbing Říp Mountain in central Bohemia (a real place), he looked down on the land below, and declared he had found their new home.

Protesters stage an anti-migrants rally in September 2015 in Prague.

There are also several minority groups in Czechia. Tensions sometimes erupt between the Czechs and the minority groups over long-standing resentments and issues of racism.

In addition, between 2001 and 2011, there was a significant uptick in the immigration of foreigners to the country. In the 2011 census, people from 182 countries were counted as residing in the Czech Republic. The most numerous group of foreigners were Ukrainians (117,810), followed by Slovaks (84,380), Vietnamese (53,110), Russians (36,055), Germans (20,780), and Poles (17,856).

ETHNIC MAKEUP

According to the official census of 2011, out of a population of approximately 10,562,000, some 63.7 percent of the people identified as ethnic Czechs,

4.9 percent claimed Moravian identity, and 1.4 percent were Slovak. A tiny 0.7 percent was made up of small groups of Poles, Germans, Romanies, and Hungarians. The remaining 26 percent were unspecified. (Please note these figures differ very slightly from the statistics listed in the *CIA World Factbook*, which is the primary source of population and demographic statistics used in this book.)

The Czech government explained the large increase in "unspecified" people by stating, "The question about nationality (that differs from the state citizenship, because it is primarily a choice made according to feelings of each person) was an optional question in the Census. While in 2001 only 173 thousand people did not want to speak about their nationality, this year already 2.74 million inhabitants used the possibility not to answer the question."

CZECH SELF-IMAGE

On the surface, the Czechs, particularly the older generation, are quite reserved and can seem unfriendly to strangers. However, with friends and relatives, they are generous and warm people. This may be explained by recent history—under Communism, people trusted only close relatives and friends, because any stranger could have been an informer for the secret police.

The younger generation, however, is especially open-minded and eager to meet new people and try new things. Czechs have a reputation for being highly cultured and intellectual with a special interest in the arts and philosophy. Optimism and confidence, however, are not strong Czech traits. This trait may be linked to their troubled history. The Czechs are similar to their Germanic neighbors—they appear to be serious, responsible, and hardworking. They are often contrasted with the Moravians and Slovaks, who are felt to be more passionate and spontaneous. Naturally these are merely generalizations, and individuals exhibit their own unique characteristics.

Czechs, in general, have been extremely sensitive about being categorized as Eastern Europeans, for they associate Eastern Europeans as backward, both socially and culturally. They are quick to point out the geographically

People in the Old Town Square in Prague gather in a circle around a musician to listen to the live music.

central location of the republic and the fact that Prague is more west than Vienna. This is perhaps one reason they were keen to be identified with Western Europe after the fall of communism.

They have a contradictory mix of high-minded ideals and very human frailties. A sociological survey of stereotypes of the Czech character found that self-traits most often mentioned by Czechs interviewed were negative: enviousness, excessive conformity, cunning, egoism, laziness, cowardice, quarrelsomeness, hypocrisy, haughtiness, and devotion to pleasure and sensuous enjoyment. Positive characteristics listed were: hardworking, skillful, and having a sense of humor. Yet when Czechs speak of themselves as a nation, they tell of a democratic, cultured, well-educated, peace-loving people. Everyday attitudes do not necessarily blemish the mythical qualities of their national character.

MINORITIES

SLOVAKS Czechs and Slovaks have shared a common national history that began after World War I and ceased with the creation of the two separate republics in 1993. Approximately 5.4 million Slovaks today live within the borders of their own independent country, Slovakia. The 2011 census, however, revealed that there were 149,000 Slovaks still living in the Czech Republic, making them one of the larger minority groups there. The Slovaks, or Slovakians, speak the Slovak language, which is closely related to the Czech language. During their recent shared history, Slovaks perceived themselves as being treated as second-class citizens by the Czechs. There is a commonly held notion among Czechs that Slovaks are the "younger brother." It is an attitude that has long inspired resentment among the Slovak minority. In spite of these feelings, there are many Czech-Slovak marriages and many Slovaks work, study, and live in the Czech Republic.

THE "LITTLE CZECH"

Czechs have a strong sense of a shared language, history, and culture, from which they derive their national identity. They refer to a mythologized persona they call the "little Czech." This "littleness" stems from the people's sense of being a small group in the midst of a much larger one, for example, Europe.

The little Czech is therefore a high achiever who is naturally very productive, but on a small scale, like a bee. He (the character is referred to as a man) is skillful, talented, and ingenious, but also the embodiment of ordinariness and common sense. He shuns high ideals and pours all his energies into his family and home. The little Czech represents the common, the ordinary, and the unexceptional. These earthy, rather than heroic, qualities, some say, are what helped Czechs survive times of oppression and foreign rule.

Others see this imaginary figure as the embodiment of all that is negative in many Czechs—Czechs, they say, are quick to point out negative traits in others, yet slow to recognize the same in themselves. As an illustration, a common Czech fable reveals the Czech character this way: When a neighbor's field has a better crop, the farmer doesn't wish for his field to yield as well as his neighbor's, but rather prays for his neighbor's crop to be ruined by blight. When his neighbor's wife buys a new fur coat, the farmer's wife doesn't desire one as well, but wishes her neighbor's coat to be eaten by moths.

POLES In 2001, some thirty-seven thousand Czech citizens claimed Polish ethnicity. The Polish community is linked mainly to the Zaolzie region in the northeastern part of the country. Many live near the town of Těšín. This is a border region that is historically ethnically mixed. Although a minority there, Poles remain a proud people with their own language, customs, festivals, radio stations, newspapers, and their own schools. There are even bilingual signs, used in certain municipalities where there are large numbers of Poles. The language they speak is a dialect called the Cieszyn Silesian, which is spoken by the majority of Poles living in the Czech Republic. It is even used by some local Czechs.

Czechs and Poles have a long history together. Even before World War I, they collaborated against German influences and movements. In 1920 the

Zaolzie region was incorporated into Czechoslovakia following an armed conflict between Poland and Czechoslovakia. In 1938 it was annexed by Poland and in 1939 by Nazi Germany. Zaolzie was returned to Czechoslovakia after World War II. During World War II, the region of Zaolzie experienced great suffering. About six thousand people died—80 percent of them were Poles.

Today, the Poles have their own Congress of Poles, set up in 1991, which represents Polish interests in the Czech Republic.

GERMANS Germans constitute one of the largest minority groups in the Czech Republic, with a population of approximately 39,000. During World War II there were 3.2 million Germans in Czech lands and Slovakia.

Germanic groups arrived in the region before the Slavs, establishing farming communities around 4000 BC. Since then, Germans have been a continuous presence in Czech history, often becoming the traditional enemy. Although the Austro-Hungarian Empire was good economically for the Czech lands, culturally it was stifling. The rulers progressively forced German language and culture onto the population until Prague and the other large Czech cities had become essentially German cities. By contrast, the German minority was treated well during the First Republic, between 1918 and 1938. The First Republic was a rich country during those two decades of peace. The Germans had their own schools and even their own university in Prague.

Nazi Germany irrevocably destroyed the social fabric in Czechoslovakia when it took possession of Sudetenland and later occupied the regions of Bohemia and Moravia. The Nazi reign of terror brought swift retaliation against all Germans after World War II, when the Czechs expelled the German minority from Czechoslovakia. Three million Germans were forced out of the country, literally overnight, leaving behind their property and lucrative businesses, especially in the industrial heartland of Bohemia. Those were expropriated by the government. Some two hundred thousand Germans died in the hardships of the march out of the country—from massacres, exhaustion, and suicide. Resentment and grievances have indelibly strained relations between the two countries. Nevertheless, in Prague on January 21, 1997, the Czech-German Declaration on Mutual Relations and their Future Development was signed—a gesture that won international praise for both nations. The declaration means that both signators agree not to allow political and legal issues from the past affect their present and future relations. Since then, it has been noted that interactions between the two countries have thawed considerably.

ROMANI The Romani, or Gyspies, are thought to be descendants of migrants from India in the fifteenth century. The Roma have been treated as inferiors throughout Europe, including the Czech Republic. Before Czechoslovakia split into two republics, there were one million Romani people in that country. Now some 13,150 people in the Czech Republic claim some Roma heritage, though only 5,199 claim to be solely Romani. Many prefer not to declare their ethnicity as Roma for fear of discrimination.

Romani people protest alleged prejudice in the Czech government.

VIETNAMESE The minorities include, interestingly, a small community of Vietnamese who run market stalls and other small businesses. They were employed during the communist era as guest workers to fill gaps in the labor market. Though no longer needed after independence, they refused to return to Vietnam, although they have since faced racism, poor working conditions, and pressure from a government that wants to send them home. Nonetheless, Czechs grudgingly admire the work ethic of their Asian guests.

TRADITIONAL CLOTHING

Folk dress grew in popularity from the 1950s due to the efforts of the communist government to revive patriotism through folkloric traditions—what they called "the people's culture." Folk songs replaced the popular tunes of the day, young people were taught folk dances and discouraged from contemporary dance forms, and May Day processions were replete with traditional dress, flags, and brass bands.

Traditional folk dress is not commonly worn every day in most parts of the republic, but older people in some villages do still wear them, and they always appear at folk festivals. Departing from the simple clothing, usually in drab colors, worn in everyday life, folk garments are embellished with bright, detailed embroidery work.

The abstract or pictorial designs and patterns vary, depending on the season and the age and marital status of the wearer. More elaborate dress evolved for church, weddings, and other special events. The attire also reflects the region—for example, in the eastern parts of the Czech Republic are seen detailed hand-sewn skirts, aprons, and shawls for men and women alike, while in the west one typically sees striking shawls, belts, headgear, and shoes.

These traditional clothes are a disappearing folk practice, barely surviving only through the efforts of minority cultural groups and others whose purpose

A young couple wears colorful traditional Czech folk costumes.

is to preserve folk culture. Most young people do not willingly participate in folk customs that call for such clothing; it certainly lacks relevance to modern, urban lifestyles. Making these clothes also leads to great expense and effort, prime reasons for abandoning the tradition.

The Chods, a group who live in a region near the German border in the northwest, are still noted for wearing traditional dress. They have lived in that place for about a thousand years, and are famous for their handicrafts, which include woodcarving and pottery. The residents make an annual pilgrimage to a mountain on the weekend following August 10, where they participate in a festival of bagpipe music and traditional song and dance.

INTERNET LINKS

http://nationalclothing.org/europe/24-czech-republic/22 -traditional-costume-of-the-czech-republic-every-region-has-its -folk-attire.html
Folk costumes of the various regions in Czechia are presented on this site.

http://www.radio.cz/en/section/panorama/in-search-of-forefather -czech-dna-tests-disclose-remote-ancestors
This is an interview with a man hoping to map the ancestral origins of the Czech people.

https://www.worldatlas.com/articles/ethnic-groups-in-the-czech -republic.html
This site provides a basic overview of ethnic groups in Czechia.

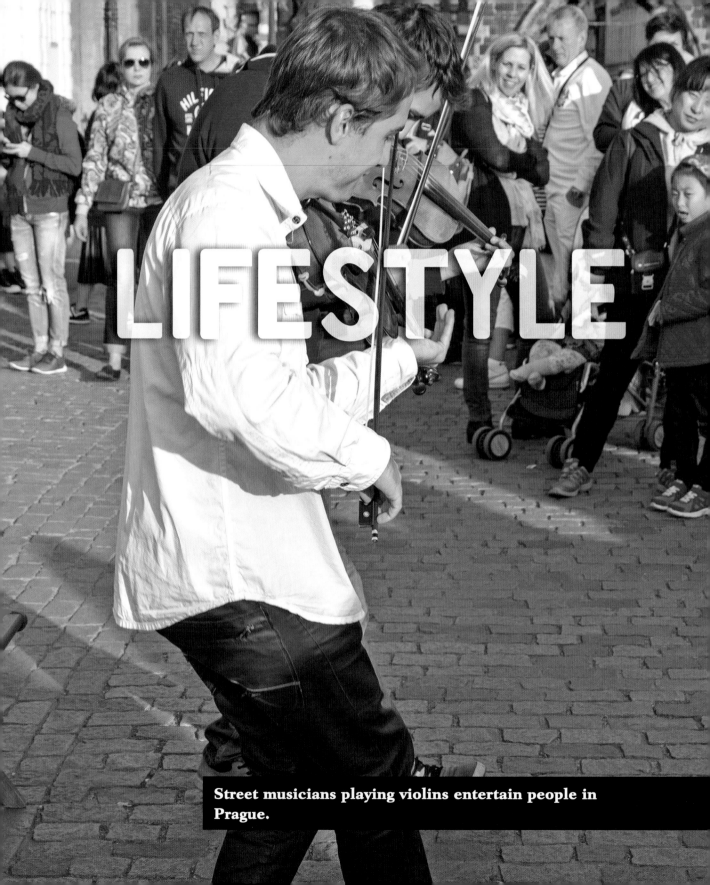

LIFESTYLE

Street musicians playing violins entertain people in Prague.

7

TRANSITIONING FROM LIFE UNDER communism to life in a free-market economy wasn't easy. The change had a huge impact on the lifestyle of the Czech people. Initially many people were reluctant to forego some of the privileges that communism once had afforded them, such as a more relaxed work routine. There was also disappointment that instant wealth for all did not follow the introduction of capitalism—which was a common misperception of life in the West at the time. There was widespread pessimism over the rising cost of living paired with inadequate income. Today, however, a measure of realism has seeped into the Czech way of life, and working people no longer expect capitalism to bestow riches upon them.

Due to its lack of international and domestic conflict, as well as its low crime rate, the Czech Republic was rated as the sixth-safest place by the 2016 Global Peace Index.

TRANSITION TO DEMOCRACY AND CAPITALISM

The Czech lifestyle has generally improved since 1989, with unemployment remaining low and the economy stable. New opportunities have been created in the workplace with the post-1989 policy of privatization and the establishment of new companies. The most progressive thinking is found in entirely new private companies. Although indifferent service was once commonplace in shops and public offices, the Czechs are now showing more courtesy and are giving good service to their customers and clients.

Life under communism was stifling, so people sought meaning and satisfaction in their lives outside of work. Family life and friendships assumed greater importance, and quiet pastimes such as stamp collecting or writing poetry were popular. The long years under a communist regime created a mentality in which people expected to get something for nothing. Today, as for many others in the Western world, life for the Czech people is more balanced. They enjoy their leisure but work hard to continue building their free-market economy.

HOW PEOPLE LIVE

About 73 percent of Czechs live in the larger towns and cities, most of them in apartments rather than houses. They tend to be very proud of their homes. Outside the apartment door or immediately inside will be a row of shoes or a cupboard for them, because Czechs usually remove their shoes at the door and put on house slippers. Their homes often have indoor plants. These are important as there is very little space in an urban setting to develop a garden. Outdoor gardening is usually done at second homes in the countryside by those who can afford them.

CITY LIVING For most Czechs, Prague is the ultimate in city living. The Czech appetite for going out and socializing is whetted by the vast number of cafés, pubs, and restaurants to be visited. It is not just about going out for a bite, however. Prague buildings display an amazing array of architectural styles and decor, which makes dining out a special occasion. The Grand Hotel

Europa, built in 1889 and then subsequently rebuilt between 1904 and 1905, is one example. The café at ground level is crowned by an oval gallery, and polished timbers gleam throughout. Here people can sit and warm their hands on a cup of delicious hot chocolate and watch others going about their business outside on the busy street in Wenceslas Square.

Prague is one of the few cities in Europe that was not bombed during World War II, consequently, it still has many beautiful old buildings. There are houses in Prague dating back to at least the early eighteenth century. Above their front doors are signs or ornamental frames made of metal, stone, or wood. These cartouches, as they are commonly called, indicated the original occupant's social rank or profession and helped to identify the building. Street numbers were introduced in 1770. Today, many Czechs continue to live in such houses, sometimes inhabiting an ancestral home that has belonged to the family for centuries.

The iconic red roofs of Prague dwarf a street festival in Old Town Square.

RURAL LIVING In old farmhouses, whether they are one-bedroom shacks or two-story buildings, activities are centered around the stove. Often there is a built-in bench right next to the stove for the little tasks that can be done while keeping warm, like darning socks or fixing a broken harness. Typically, the area around the stove is covered in strikingly colored ceramic tiles. Near the stove and along the wall hang enamel pots. If the house has a second story, the main bedroom is located directly above the stove in order to take advantage of its rising warmth.

Many country dwellings are constructed of wood. The surface of a wall is often decorated with strips of wood arranged in patterns, providing texture and interest. Window frames have elaborate designs. Individual preferences for ornamentation is also shown in wardrobes, chests of drawers, and other furniture, which are typically painted with elaborate patterns, both abstract and figurative. Hand-embroidered bedcovers contrast beautifully

A traditional timbered cottage is decorated in the Czech style.

with the dark tones of the wooden head- and footboards. Czechs enjoy the simple pleasures of their country homes, especially as weekend or vacation retreats. They deeply appreciate the stillness and beauty of the countryside.

THE FAMILY

A nuclear family of parents and their children is the basic Czech family unit, while the bond between extended family members is generally lifelong, too. Although people, particularly the younger generation, relocate more often than in the past for work reasons, contact between siblings after marriage remains constant.

Statues of Babička and her grandchildren pay tribute to Božena Němcová's famous book.

In many families, *Babička* (BAB-ich-ka), or the grandmother, is the key figure. Grandmothers enjoy much respect as a source of wisdom, but they also are figures of authority. They often serve as babysitters, or live with the young parents, as it is common for both parents to work. The legendary status of the grandmother is described in the 1855 novel *Babička*, by Božena Němcová, which is an all-time favorite with Czechs of all ages.

THE ROLE OF WOMEN

A 2013 report by the European Commission found that about 57 percent of Czech women age fifteen to sixty-four work outside the home. Only 8.5 percent work part-time. Most work in manufacturing (18.4 percent), wholesale and retail (11.5 percent), or health care and social work (11.2 percent). About 8 percent work in education fields. Women tend to work in more traditionally female roles, such as legal, social, and cultural professionals; personal service workers; general and keyboard clerks; and sales workers. Czech men, by contrast, work in more typically male sectors, such as metal and machinery trades, construction trades, as drivers, and as science and engineering professionals. The average female employee earns 25.5 percent less than the average male employee.

The discussion of women's rights surfaced in Czech society only after 1989. The first public debate on feminism was broadcast on television in 1992, and a single book that was hailed as the first Czech feminist writing was published that year, too.

In the Czech Republic today, "feminism" can be seen as a "dirty" word, even among women who support gender equality. Most Czech women prefer not to call themselves feminists. To some extent, feminism is misunderstood as a radical, anti-male movement imported from the West. Part of the reason for this may be the legacy of socialist policies. Under the communist regime, women's entitlements already included equal pay for equal work, equal educational opportunities, and six months' maternity leave at full pay. Nurseries and kindergartens were provided in local communities and in the workplace. Public institutions employed a greater number of women than in the West because of gender quotas set by the government.

Detractors of communist ideology argue that socialism actually exploited women. By placing women in the workforce, many Czech families became accustomed to having two incomes, instead of just one. Women, however, were expected to continue to shoulder the traditional responsibilities of home and children. Despite the law on equal pay, 45 percent of women surveyed in 1991 reported their pay to be less than that of men for the same kind of work, and women were more likely to be fired.

Many Czechs do not challenge certain premises that influence and restrict any trend toward real gender equality. They see gender differences as embedded in nature, resulting directly from the biological differences between men and women. Many women emphasize their unique experience of childbearing, and both men and women argue that most women's desires are almost entirely focused on the bearing and raising of children.

Czech women today are primarily concerned with greater representation in politics, so that they themselves can address issues such as education, child benefits, child care, maternity benefits, and other family policy and family law issues. Many women also believe that the presence of women in parliament would lead to more compassionate and honest government.

WEDDINGS AND MARRIAGE

Traditionally, Czechs tended to marry young, especially in rural areas. A girl unmarried at twenty-two might be thought of as "on the shelf." Traditionally, girls were pressured to "catch" a man before he went off to complete his military service, but such pressures are declining and compulsory military service no longer applies. Folk customs are still part of village weddings. Elaborately embroidered clothes are worn, special songs and dances performed, and old rituals such as the mock abduction of the bride are also reenacted.

A bridal couple poses with family on their wedding day.

However, traditional social patterns began changing in the early 1990s. Today, Czechs tend to marry less often and later. More remain single, and many prefer cohabitation over marriage. The divorce rate has increased to nearly 50 percent—meaning almost half of all marriages fall apart—with the average Czech marriage lasting thirteen years. Compared to other countries in the European Union, the Czech Republic has one of the highest divorce rates.

Women are also postponing having their first child until they are older. In 2000, most Czech women had their first child at age twenty-four, while in 2013—a mere thirteen years later—the average age was twenty-nine. The customary tradition of marriage first, then children also turned around, so that the trend now is to have a child first, then get married. Nevertheless, more than half of the population aged twenty and over is married.

Many Czechs want to see that privilege extended to same-sex couples. In March 2006, the parliament overturned a veto by President Václav Klaus to have the Czech Republic become the first former communist country in Europe to grant legal recognition to same-sex partnerships. That recognition, however, is not the same as marriage. Prior to the October 2017 election, a coalition of five Czech organizations kicked off a campaign called *Jsme fér!,* ("We are fair!" or "It's only fair!") aimed at achieving marriage equality during the following four-year parliamentary period. At that time, a poll found 52 percent of Czechs in favor of marriage equality. As of January 2018, the Czech Republic does not allow same-sex marriage, but the tide may be turning.

A LITERATE PEOPLE

Education in primary and secondary schools, from ages six to sixteen, is compulsory, and continues to be fully funded by the state. There are also state kindergartens for children aged three to six and secondary schools preparing students aged fifteen to eighteen for university. The literacy rate is around 99 percent, with 97 percent of Czechs progressing to secondary education and 50 percent enrolled in tertiary, or higher, education. Tuition at a state university is free and the state pays health insurance for students up to twenty-six years of age.

Czechs consider themselves to be educated people, and statistics back up their perceptions. They revere education and encourage their children to do well academically. The republic has many universities and other institutes of higher learning. The main ones are the Charles University and the Czech Technical University in Prague, the Masaryk University in Brno, the Palacký University in Olomouc and the Liberec University of Technology.

Expenditure on education is about 4.1 percent of GDP (in 2013), according the World Bank. The average school-life expectancy from primary through tertiary education is sixteen years for males and eighteen years for female students.

HEALTH CARE

Czech health service has undergone drastic transformation after the political changes in 1989. The national health system was dismantled and freedom of choice of health care was adopted in 1990 and 1991. Major reforms have included the decentralization and liberalization of the health care system.

Czechs enjoy universal health care coverage in which they can choose their own doctor. The country has one of the world's highest ratios of physicians to citizens. In 1992 a compulsory health insurance system was introduced, based on individual contributions. Those are paid by individuals and by employers or by the state.

In 2016, the Europe Health Consumer Index ranked healthcare in the Czech Republic to be the 13th most successful out of thirty-five European countries, just after Sweden, and two places ahead of the United Kingdom, with the Netherlands coming in at first place.

INTERNET LINKS

http://ceenewperspectives.iir.cz/2017/06/21/lgbt-community-in -czech-republic-tolerance-or-indifference
This article looks at the present state of attitudes toward LGBT issues and marriage equality in the Czech Republic.

http://ec.europa.eu/justice/gender-equality/files/epo_campaign /country_profile_czech_republic_en.pdf
Gender equality in Czech Republic is the subject of this report.

http://www.euro.who.int/__data/assets/pdf_file/0005/280706 /Czech-HiT.pdf?ua=1
Detailed information on the Czech healthcare system can be found in this 2015 report.

http://www.mzv.cz/dublin/en/about_the_czech_republic/education_ in_the_czech_republic
The Czech Embassy provides an overview of the country's education system.

RELIGION

Crowds surround the historic Saint Nicholas Church in
Old Town Square in Prague.

8

THE MANY CHURCHES AND cathedrals that dot the Czech Republic's landscape are testament to the country's religious past. However, the oppressive communist regime (1948—1989) turned many Czechs away from any sort of religious beliefs. Once a primarily Catholic nation, it is now one of the least religious in Europe.

More than half (51.9 percent) of the population claims to be unaffiliated with a religion, and more than one third (34.2 percent) are agnostics or nonbelievers. Only 10.3 percent belong to the Roman Catholic Church, and less than 1 percent of the people belong to each of several churches, such as the Evangelical Christian and the Czechoslovak Hussite Christian churches. Buddhist and Muslim communities are tiny. In fact, the Czech Republic has the fewest Muslims of all other countries in the European Union.

THE CHRISTIAN EMISSARIES

The Greek monks Cyril and Methodius, who were brothers, brought Christianity to the Slavic lands in 860 CE. Their work in Central and Eastern Europe involved translating the Bible into the various local spoken languages. Cyril, the younger of the two, was educated at a school for children of the Byzantine imperial family. He had a gift for languages and held prestigious positions as professor of philosophy

In the most recent census in 2011, more than fifteen thousand people in the Czech Republic listed their religion as "Knights of the Jedi," in a reference to the Star Wars movies. Listing one's religion as Jedi was apparently a way to protest the inclusion of a religion category on the national census, but some folks claim the Jedi religion to be real.

A statue of Saints Cyril and Methodius on the summit of Radhošť Mountain is a popular pilgrimage destination.

at the Magnaura Palace School and as librarian of Saint Sofia Cathedral in Constantinople (modern Istanbul). The Greek missionary brothers belonged to the Orthodox Christian Church of Constantinople. In the Czech area they translated the Bible into the Slavic language of the time, causing much controversy because it was seen as heretical to teach Christianity in any language other than one of the then holy languages—Greek, Latin, and Hebrew. Cyril had to invent an alphabet to do this, and a later form of it became the widely used Cyrillic alphabet.

As part of the Holy Roman Empire, Bohemians and Moravians remained loyal to the Catholic faith until the reformer and philosopher Jan Hus (yahn HOOS) (1369—1415) agitated against what he saw as corruption in the church and a need to return to early Christian principles. Hus was burned as a heretic in 1415, and his followers, a politico-religious group called the Hussites, started the Hussite Wars that raged from 1419 to 1434. The Hussites were divided into two groups: the Taborites and the Utraquists. Utraquists take their name from their doctrine of the double communion—they receive both bread and wine. The Latin *utraque* means "each of two."

The Taborites merged with another group called the Bohemian Brethren in 1457; some Utraquists merged with the Lutherans and others with the Roman Catholics. Czechs remained strongly Protestant for two more centuries, although the country was part of the Holy Roman Empire.

In the seventeenth century, the Hapsburg Empire rose to prominence in the Czech lands, bringing with it religious intolerance. Catholicism was forced upon the Protestant Czechs, particularly after their defeat in the Battle of the White Mountain in 1620. The religious freedom that was enjoyed after Czechoslovakia was formed in 1918 lasted for a relatively brief period. A communist government came into power in 1948, proclaiming the state officially atheist, closing most churches and jailing many members of the clergy. In response, some devout Czechs started an underground religious network that conducted services in secret and had links to the political underground movement.

An engraving of Jan Hus

In January 1977, more than two hundred prominent Czech intellectuals produced a manifesto called Charter 77, which was a document committed to human rights. Signatories included the famous playwrights Václav Havel and Pavel Kohout. Many of the signatories were arrested and denounced by the Czech authorities following the publication of the manifesto.

Czechs regained their religious freedom with the introduction of a tolerant and democratic constitution in 1990. Almost every Christian group is represented in the republic, as are other religions, including Judaism, Islam, Buddhism, and Hare Krishna, a movement of the Hindu faith. In each case, however, the communities are quite small.

FADING CHRISTIANITY

Czechs do not attend church services regularly. It is mostly the elderly who go to church at all these days, although increasing numbers of children attend religious education classes. People do not generally discuss religious matters, as they are considered irrelevant to daily life. Despite their reduced congregations, churches in larger cities are still crowded because of the many tourists interested in them.

There appears to be a reluctance among Czechs to be expressive Christians. Some Czechs have warned of the danger of the Catholic Church becoming authoritarian and hence undemocratic.

The Catholic Church has been compensated by the government for church property the communist government confiscated in the past. Part of those funds has gone toward restoring and maintaining Catholic churches throughout the country. There are now many beautiful old churches in the countryside as well as in the cities.

St. Barbara's Church is in the center of Kutná Hora, which is a UNESCO World Heritage Site.

The Protestants are represented by several groups in the Czech Republic, the largest being the Evangelical Church of Czech Brethren, with about 52,000 members.

Although many Czechs are not devout Christians in practice, Czechs in general believe in a moral upbringing for their children that will guide them into responsible citizenship with a civic sense of duty. The notion of a civil society is close to the heart of most Czechs. They revere their first president, Tomáš Garrigue Masaryk, for his philosophical background and his ardent support of democracy and tolerance.

JUDAISM

The presence of Jews in the Czech lands began in the eleventh century, with thriving communities and businesses in Prague. In the thirteenth century, however, the Roman Catholic Church decreed that Jews and Christians should live separately. The

Hastalska Street in the Josefov, or Jewish Quarter, in the Old Town district of Prague

Jews were crowded into a walled ghetto. Jews in the Czech lands have been alternately welcomed and persecuted for several centuries—welcomed because they were successful traders and craftsmen and paid lucrative taxes, yet persecuted by mobs and rulers alike and forced to defend their synagogues and private property from sanctioned plunder. Under Empress Maria Theresa (reigned 1740–1780), Jews were exiled from Prague and forced to pay special taxes. Her son, Emperor Joseph II (r. 1780–1790), decreed religious tolerance, but it was partly because he needed more money from able taxpayers. He ordered the ghetto walls torn down, and the Jewish quarter was made a borough of Prague. It was named Josefov in his honor.

Czech Jews who survived World War II sorrowfully remember another ghetto, Theresienstadt (modern Terezín), which was created by the Germans as a "distribution camp" to sort the trainloads of Jews before passing them on to concentration camps. From Prague alone, forty thousand Jews made their final journey to this ghetto. Anti-Semitism was a characteristic of the communist regime also, although it was not as lethal as that promoted by Hitler. Unfortunately, anti-Semitism continues in the Czech Republic today.

Less than four thousand Jews remain in the Czech Republic today. The largest Jewish community continues to be located in the Josefov quarter of Prague. There are smaller communities in Brno and Ostrava.

In 1997 Czech leaders finally agreed to compensate Slovak Jews for gold and other valuables that the fascist regime had confiscated from Slovak Holocaust victims in World War II. The valuables had been deposited in the Czechoslovak State Bank in 1953 and assimilated into the federal budget. Approximately $590,000 was paid into a foundation run by Jewish organizations. The Czech government paid two-thirds of the total and the Slovak government the rest.

PLACES OF WORSHIP

The long history of Christianity and Judaism in the Czech Republic has resulted in the erection of beautiful and architecturally significant places of worship. Prague boasts some of the best known among them, including Saint Vitus Cathedral. Located in the heart of Hradčany (ha-rad-CHA-nay), the cathedral's foundation stone was laid in 1344 by Charles IV, but the cathedral was not completed until 1929, when a concerted effort was made to finish the work during the Czech National Revival Movement. Consequently, it is a mixture of Gothic, Renaissance, and Baroque styles. The doorways are richly decorated with carvings of historical and biblical scenes, and the interior is illuminated by traditional and modern stained glass windows. Unfortunately, it is among Prague's many stately and important buildings in dire need of renovation and cleaning to rid its blackened surface of the effects of aging and pollution.

In Josefov, half a dozen original synagogues remain standing. The Old-New Synagogue is Europe's oldest synagogue. The main part was built in 1270, and women's prayer galleries were added in the seventeenth century. Some features of the synagogue that resembled symbols of Christian churches have been destroyed. Other synagogues in Josefov have been refitted into museums to exhibit sacred Jewish artifacts, many of which were rescued from demolished Bohemian synagogues. Such beloved places dedicated to their culture and religion are of great significance to Jews of the Czech Republic and others everywhere. Ironically, they were spared by Hitler from destruction so that they might be used as part of his "museum of an extinct race."

The Old New Synagogue in Josefov, Praque, is Europe's oldest active synagogue.

INTERNET LINKS

https://www.theguardian.com/commentisfree/belief/2010/jun/24/czech-republic-religious-atheism
This article discusses the state of Czech's spiritual beliefs.

http://www.pewresearch.org/fact-tank/2017/06/19/unlike-their-central-and-eastern-european-neighbors-most-czechs-dont-believe-in-god
A 2015—2016 study by the Pew Research Center provides information on religious attitudes in Czech Republic and neighboring countries.

LANGUAGE

A road sign in central Prague points the way to important locations.

9

C ZECHS ARE PROUD OF THEIR language, which they have had to defend against foreign rulers. They see themselves as cultured and educated people, and the fastidious way they use their language reflects those attributes. Language is deeply interwoven with a country's culture, civilization, and identity, and that is certainly the case in the Czech Republic.

Czech is spoken by more than ten million people. It is written in the roman script, as is English. Above some vowels and consonants are accent marks that determine pronunciation.

Czech is a complex language where nouns are accorded a gender; for example, table in Czech is masculine, book is feminine, and bicycle is neuter. It is also a highly inflected language, which is to say that the word meanings subtly change according to usage, conjugation, and pronunciation. The ending of a noun depends on what role the noun plays in the sentence (is it the subject doing an action, or is it the object?), while the ending of a verb depends on its tense: present, past, or future.

ANCIENT ROOTS

Most modern European, Middle Eastern, and Indian languages are derived from the family of languages called Indo-European. Czech

The US Foreign Institute ranks the world's languages into four categories according to their difficulty for Americans to learn. Arabic, Cantonese and Mandarin Chinese, Japanese, and Korean make up Category 4, the most difficult ("super-hard") languages. Czech is rated as a Category 3 ("hard") language, along with forty-nine other languages in that category.

Here are some surprising and interesting things about the Czech language.

- *Some Czech words have no vowels. For example,* prst *means "finger,"* čtvrt *is "quarter," and* krk *means "neck."*

- *Spoken Czech has a sound that exists in no other language, which linguists call the raised alveolar non-sonorant trill. This special kind of rolled R is the letter Ř in the Czech alphabet. Most non-native speakers find it almost impossible to make this sound. It's a voiceless vibration that sounds something like a helicopter flying overhead, or a motorcycle at idle. This trill is made by putting the tongue against the roof of the mouth just behind the front teeth and vibrating it.*

- *The word* robot *was invented by a Czech writer. Derived from the Czech word* robotnik (serf), robot *was coined by Czech novelist and playwright Karel Čapek in his play,* Rossum's Universal Robots, *in 1921, to describe a machine-made man, an automaton. Words are often borrowed from one language and absorbed into another.* Polka *and* pistol *are Czech words that settled comfortably into English.*

belongs to one branch of that group, Common Slavonic. Czech is closely related to Slovak and to a lesser extent, Polish. In fact, the older generation of Czechs and Slovaks, who lived in Czechoslovakia, can easily understand each other. This is not the case, however, among the younger generation, which has not been as exposed to each other's language.

The Slavic groups that settled in the Czech lands had evolved a common language as early as the ninth century. In 860, two Byzantine monks, the brothers Cyril and Methodius, translated the Bible into the Czech local language and thus a written form of Slavonic was produced for the first time.

THE LANGUAGE EVOLVES

In the Middle Ages, Old Church Slavonic was replaced by Latin, the language of medieval European learning. That was followed by the consolidation of

German in the Bohemian kingdom, as many rulers of that period were German. The establishment of Charles University in Prague in 1348, by the Czech king and Holy Roman emperor Charles IV, fostered the development of the Czech language. It was the first university to be built in Central Europe.

After their defeat in the Thirty Years' War (1618–1648), Czechs were once again dominated by a foreign civilization. They lost their rights as citizens, and German replaced the Czech language in the public affairs of the region. Czech culture and literature were stifled, but the spoken language survived in the countryside, where peasants continued to use their own language. This led to a social barrier between the lower and rural classes on one side and the noble and urban classes on the other.

Josef Dobrovsky

In the nineteenth century, Josef Dobrovský (1753–1829), a Jesuit priest and scholar, wrote a systematic grammar of the Czech language. Later, František Palacký (1798–1876), a historian and politician, published a history of Bohemia, a work in five volumes written between 1836 and 1867. Both writers were important in establishing Czech lands and language amid the European community of nations.

In the late nineteenth century, nationalistic sentiments took off across the continent, and language became a crucial issue. Recognizing the need to assert their own cultural heritage, Czechs demanded the freedom to speak and write in their own language. They succeeded in 1918, when the independent Republic of Czechoslovakia was formed. Since then, the Czech language has not faced any real threat except during World War II, when the Nazis shut down institutions of learning. Later, under the communists, learning Russian as a second language was made compulsory in schools.

FOREIGN INFLUENCES

It is inevitable that the German language continues to play a role in the Czech Republic, especially as the nation shares a border with Germany. Germanisms are present in the border dialects and in colloquial language. In the past, young male Czechs would travel to German-speaking areas in search of apprenticeships, returning speaking fluent German, while girls often went into domestic service in German-speaking Austrian households. Despite tensions, Germans and Austrians remain Czechs' closest contact with the Western world. It is therefore expedient for Czechs, especially those in the service industries, to speak German, and Germans are widely sought as customers and business partners.

Since the Velvet Revolution of 1989, foreign investment has been encouraged by the Czech government. There was also a widespread acknowledgement that Czechs needed foreigners to join their companies to teach local workers new skills and impart knowledge. As a result, the English language has also established a foothold in the country, primarily

NEVYBUCHLÁ MUNICE
NEBEZPEČÍ OHROŽENÍ ŽIVOTA!
BLINDGÄNGER LEBENSGEFAHR!
UNEXPLODED MUNITION
DANGER!

A sign in the old military area of Šumava National Park, on the Czech border with Germany and Austria, warns of unexploded munitions in three languages.

FORMS OF ADDRESS

As every noun in Czech has a gender, surnames differ depending on whether they are male or female. The wife of a man whose surname is Navrátil would be known as Navrátilová. Czechs address one another with the honorary titles of Pan *(PAHN, Mister),* Paní *(PA-ni, Missus), and* Slečna *(SLE-tchna, Miss). Titles such as "doctor" and "professor" for teachers are also used. Forms of address combine the primary form (Pan, Paní, Slečna), with other titles, for example, "Pan Doctor Navratil."*

Shaking hands is customary upon meeting someone. Even people in a hurry will reach out to clasp each other's hands momentarily. Close friends also exchange kisses on both cheeks, men and women alike.

in the major cities, in the areas of tourism and business. Many expatriate Britons, Americans, and Irish working in the cities are active in the republic's campaign to replace Russian with English as the foreign language of choice, and language schools eagerly employ native English speakers. The campaign has been successful, and language schools offering English continue to thrive.

This situation may have reached a plateau in the business world, where private companies are employing fewer foreign workers as more Czechs workers have been brought up-to-date. Many help wanted ads in major newspapers, especially in Prague, however, continue to request bilingual Czech/English speakers. Czechs have quickly come to realize the prominence of the English language in the rest of Europe. Because they were forced to learn Russian at school under the communist regime as their first foreign language, many Czechs can still speak Russian but choose not to.

INTERNET LINKS

https://www.britannica.com/topic/Czech-language
This site gives a history of the language.

https://www.omniglot.com/writing/czech.htm
This site provides a good overview to Czech language with many related links.

ARTS

A statue of Antonin Dvořák stands outside the Rudolfinum, the main concert hall in Prague.

10

FROM THE BLOWN GLASS OF Bohemia to the traditional bagpipe music of the Chodsko region to the architectural beauty of Prague, the Czechs have expressed a strong affinity for the arts throughout their history. Their buildings are magnificent examples of Gothic, Renaissance, and Baroque styles; Czech composers, writers, dramatists, and craftsmen have enriched the world stage; and literary and musical festivals are esteemed annual events.

MUSIC

Czech musical traditions date far back in history. The Arab explorer Ibrahim ibn Jakub described string and woodwind instruments used by the Slavs in the region of Bohemia in 965 CE. A rare eleventh- or twelfth-century lute is the earliest intact instrument found in that region. Four fourteenth-century hymns in the Czech language have also been discovered.

The fifteenth-century Hussite Movement (named after religious reformer Jan Hus) was responsible for the creation of distinctive Czech hymns. Folk music developed swiftly after that and is still enjoyed in

"Co Čech, to muzikant" is a common Czech expression that means something like "Every Czech is a musician." If not literally so, it is nevertheless true that the Czech Republic is an exceptionally musical nation, which has produced several world class artists and composers.

villages today. That early spurt was followed by a period of stagnation when Czech music survived only at the village level, or was kept alive by Czech emigrants, such as the composer Jan Dismas Zelenka, who worked in Dresden in the eighteenth century.

The nineteenth century was a rich and productive time. Bedřich Smetana (1824—1884), believed to be the first nationalist Czech composer, departed from traditional melodies in composing his operas and symphonic poems. His best-known works include *The Brandenburgers in Bohemia* and *The Bartered Bride*. He lost his hearing in 1874. Over the next five years he wrote a cycle of six symphonic poems, collectively called *Má Vlast* ("*My Country*"), about Bohemia. Hearing one of them, *Vltava* ("*The Moldau*"), a listener follows the course of the river beside which Smetana spent many hours completing his compositions.

While Smetana laid the foundation of nationalist music, Antonín Dvořák (1841—1904), who played second viola in Smetana's orchestra, developed this theme and left an abundant legacy—thirty-one works of chamber music, fourteen string quartets, fifty orchestral works, and nine symphonies.

Dvořák started his musical career playing the violin in his father's inn and paid his own way through a two-year music course in Prague. In 1875 he met the German composer Johannes Brahms, whose friendship and patronage led to the publication of Dvořák's *Moravian Duets* (1876) and *Slavonic Dances* (1878). Dvořák achieved fame in England for his choral music and was made director of the National Conservatory of Music in New York in 1892; the three years he spent in New York City resulted in his *Symphony No. 9 "From the New World."* Despite his fame abroad, he remained a humble, religious family man, who was most at home in the Bohemian countryside.

Leoš Janáček (1854—1928), another nationalist composer who was a contemporary of Smetana and Dvořák, was born in Moravia. He founded a college for organists in Brno in 1881 and was its director for almost forty years. Janáček composed choral music as well as chamber and orchestral works, and much of his work is based on traditional folk music. He was particularly skilled in manipulating his music for dramatic effect. Among his internationally famous operas are *The Cunning Little Vixen* and *From the House of the Dead*. *Kat'a Kabanová* is an opera that grew out of his interest in Russian language and literature.

ARTISANS OF BOHEMIA Early eighteenth century Bohemia was known as the conservatory of Europe as, increasingly, Bohemian artists and composers were establishing themselves all over Europe. Their exuberant musical heritage is footed partly in the Bohemian tradition of hand making violins and lutes, a stringed instrument with a large pear-shaped body and rich tones.

Lute making preceded violin making by several centuries. Plucked instruments predominated because, until the early seventeenth century, singing rather than instrumental music was the fashion, and it was easier to sing to a lute than to a bowed instrument. The use of lutes dates back to at least the thirteenth century, and the lute is illustrated in Jan Amos Comenius's 1658 *Orbis Sensualium Pictus* ("The World in Pictures").

Many Bohemian Protestants emigrated to other German-speaking lands to sidestep the forced Catholicization of their country after 1620. Once settled, they established some of the earliest craft guilds ever recorded.

Ironically, the religious and political changes wrought by the devastation of the Thirty Years' War provided the impetus to the development of music in general. The Roman Catholic Church established closer ties with the populace and raised grand churches and provided religious ceremonies in them for which musicians could compose music. In this setting, stringed instruments found their niche. This fertile period, the Baroque, was a high point in musical development.

The latter half of the seventeenth century saw the arrival of many talented immigrants from Germany and Tyrol, a region of Austria. Most such artisans established themselves in Prague and formed guilds. That infusion of expertise in making violins provided a stimulus to the local artisans. Typically, a master of the craft would open up a shop. His sons would be introduced to the craft from an early age, learning as apprentices, and would continue the family tradition.

During the National Revival Movement (late eighteenth and nineteenth centuries), Czech craftsmen began to leave Prague to work in smaller towns. The humble beginnings of a group of skilled workers who were to become Czech masters appeared in a small town called Passkey, in the hills dividing northern Bohemia from German Silesia. Věnceslav Metelka, a joiner and self-taught violin maker, trained his sons and daughter in the trade. A school established itself there over time, with more family members becoming artisans and taking on pupils. The Metelka family is but one example of the long-standing traditions of musical artisanship that became embedded in the national psyche. The Czechs can rightly claim that musical prowess runs in their veins—at least, metaphorically.

The violins made in these traditional shops varied in shape and curve, the type of woods used, the size and angles of the holes, the quality of the acoustics, and even the color and formulas of the wood varnish. Many violin makers placed labels with their names on their products, although often the name of the shop owner rather than the apprentice would appear on the finished instrument. Many of those men were musicians as well, and had a deep affinity with their craft. At about this time, too, the working class began to develop an interest in cultural pursuits, and many locally made violins found their way into middle-class homes.

DRAMA

Czech drama goes back to pre-Christian times when festivals included theatrical performances. In the thirteenth century, plays had themes taken from daily life. By the sixteenth century Czech-language theater had established itself, and its themes were mainly biblical. At Charles University in Prague, plays were performed in Latin and were used as a method of teaching. After the Thirty Years' War, the Czech-language theater vanished, reappearing only more than a century later, in Prague.

The First Czechoslovak Republic supported new works in theater. In contrast, the communist period after World War II welcomed the production of good classical theater, but hardly any modern productions. Plays produced by dissident playwrights such as Václav Havel—later to be elected president—were banned because of their antigovernment bias. The Western world gained access to them, though, so the work of the dissidents became known outside their own country. The mid to late 1960s provided a respite from government censorship, and consequently, free expression was explored in Prague's theaters, such as the Theater by the Railings, which was founded in 1958.

Since the overthrow of communism, new theater groups have flowered. The Czech Republic plays host to an annual international theater festival, which draws enthusiastic crowds. Theatergoing is a passion for many Czechs, especially the elderly.

PUPPET THEATER Marionette plays have been popular since the sixteenth century, their demand peaking in the seventeenth and early eighteenth centuries. They were considered children's entertainment until a revival in the twentieth century. Josef Skupa's legendary puppets, Spejbl and Hurvínek, created in the 1920s, still perform in Prague. Puppetry festivals are held throughout the country each year. The Museum of Puppet Art in Prague hosts shows daily and has the largest collection in the world.

The beloved puppets Spejbl and Hurvínek are on display in Prague.

FOLK ARTS AND CRAFTS

Dressed in traditional costumes, musicians perform at a folklore festival in Prague.

Much of the physical evidence of Czech folk traditions reaches back only to the nineteenth-century National Revival Movement, because of the perishable nature of most materials, such as wood and clay. Folk arts take the forms of stories, songs, music, dance, clothing, and architectural styles. Those traditions have been preserved to this day in families, passing from each generation to a younger one, or publicly, through museums and festivals. Folk festivals usually occur in the summer or fall. They provide occasions for neighbors to gather and enjoy themselves with music and dancing and the wearing of traditional folk dress. The sleepy town of Strážnice (STRAJ-nitse), for example, suddenly springs to life at the end of June for the International Folklore Festival. Participants from all over Europe take part in spirited competitions.

FOLK MUSEUMS All over the countryside are open-air museums called *skansens* (SKAN-suhn) that incorporate traditional architecture and furnishings. Some are sites of folk festivals, and the better ones attempt to show not only single buildings but also the way entire communities lived. For that purpose, barns, churches, homes, and other buildings have been transported piece by piece and filled with utensils, linen, furniture, and clothing typical of the period.

LITERATURE

The earliest Czech literary works were hymns and religious texts in Old Church Slavonic and tenth-century legends of Saint Wenceslas. Jan Hus's *Orthographia Bohemica* was among the religious tracts of the fourteenth century. Themes of morality and chronicles of daily life and of journeys were featured in sixteenth- and seventeenth-century prose. The persecution of secular scholars since the seventeenth century discouraged local creative writing for about two centuries.

BOHEMIAN CRYSTAL

A legend tells of an old woman walking through the Giant Mountains carrying a basket of newly made glassware to market. She slipped and fell, smashing her goods to pieces. Devastated though she was, she listened to Krakonoš, the spirit of the mountains, who commanded her to take her basket of shattered glass home. Upon her arrival, she found that the broken glass had been transformed into gold!

Czechs, especially Bohemians, have been discovering gold in the trade of cut and engraved glass and crystal for several centuries. In the second half of the seventeenth century, the small trade of glass cutting and engraving formally established itself into guilds. As interest in decorated glass grew, Bohemian craftsmen developed a rock crystal type of glass, which expanded the range of possible decoration. Limestone was the key ingredient in this glass, giving it greater brilliance and providing a still more striking contrast against the matte engraving.

By the end of the seventeenth century, the knowledge of how to make limestone crystal glass had spread throughout Bohemia and reached other parts of Europe. Bohemian glass began to be exported, and by the end of the eighteenth century was known in most of Europe, the Middle East, and the Americas. Engravers found inspiration in many sources—biblical tales, images on coins and maps, and the landscape around them. Bohemian artisans also traveled widely with their wares and customized their products to buyers' requests.

Glass and crystal continue to be produced in Bohemia today. As with most crafts that began before the industrial revolution, glass cutting and engraving have grown into an industry based on mass production. The days when only the nobility were able to afford such beautiful objects are gone. Engraved glass and crystal are now affordable commodities.

From the mid-nineteenth to the early twentieth centuries, Czech writers developed nationalistic and political themes. Among the writers of that period are Jaroslav Hašek (1883—1923) and Karel Čapek (1890—1938). Hašek, a practical joker, had a colorful career—he was, in turn, bank clerk, newspaper editor (by age twenty-one), soldier in World War I, prisoner of war of the Russians, and communist propagandist for the Bolsheviks before turning to writing full time. Best known for *The Good Soldier* (Švejk), a satire on military life, Hašek's novels made fun of authoritarian regimes. Čapek, a Czech novelist, playwright, and essayist, explored morality in his works. He often collaborated with his brother Josef, a dramatist and illustrator, in writing plays.

Early in the same period, Jan Neruda (1834—1891) wrote popular light fiction about nineteenth-century Prague. Two famous collections of his are *Tales of the Lesser Quarter* and *Pictures of Old Prague.*

There used to be a strong Czech tradition of writing in German. An influential Austrian group known as the Prague Circle included Jewish fiction writer Franz Kafka (1883—1924), novelist, poet, and playwright Franz Werfel (1890—1945), and the poet Rainer Maria Rilke (1875—1926). When World War II ended, the German minority was expelled, and that linguistic tradition ended abruptly.

Communism dampened the literary spirit; the 1950s turned out writing in the socialist realist style. Nevertheless, the Prague Spring of the 1960s saw a flowering of writing with authors such as Milan Kundera. After the invasion of Warsaw Pact troops in 1968, Kundera was among the writers who were forced to leave the country in order to continue their work.

POETIC TENDENCIES Czech poetry is not popularly read in other countries because it is difficult to translate and interpret. Karel Hynek Mácha (1810—1836) is considered the greatest nineteenth-century Czech poet. He was greatly influenced by English and Polish Romantic literature, and his lyrical epic *Máj* (May) has been highly praised by twentieth-century poets and critics. Mácha tragically died of pneumonia just before his twenty-sixth birthday.

Jaroslav Seifert (1901—86) was a journalist until 1950, then a freelance writer. His poetry reflects the momentous events of the German occupation of Czechoslovakia, the Soviet coup of 1948, and the liberation of the Prague Spring. His poetry and articles lost publishers because of his opposition to the Soviet invasion. His themes ranged from patriotism to political critiques. His work began to be republished in the Czech Republic in 1979. Jaroslav Seifert won the Nobel Prize in Literature in 1984.

PAINTING

Early examples of painting in the Czech lands include illuminated manuscripts and church frescoes of the Romanesque period and Byzantine paintings in the late thirteenth century. Book illumination was the dominant form of painting during the late Gothic and Renaissance periods.

Reverie (1898) by Alphonse Mucha epitomizes the artist's dreamy, decorative style.

Czech realism flowered during the later stages of the revival movement in the nineteenth century when subject matters dealt mostly with the prosaic. An era of landscape art was followed by Impressionism and Symbolism.

Art Nouveau became very popular in the late nineteenth and early twentieth centuries. Many Czech artists were inspired by the Art Nouveau styles of Paris. Among them was Alphonse Mucha (1860—1939), famed for his delicate female figures whose hair and clothing merged with the background in elaborate, decorative detail. He achieved fame for his posters advertising French actress Sarah Bernhardt in her many roles. In his later travels to the United States, he met Chicago industrialist Charles Richard Crane, who sponsored twenty large historical paintings in the series "Epic of the Slavic People," which Mucha painted between 1912 and 1930. They were given to the city of Prague.

Surrealism inspired Czech artists in the early twentieth century and continues to be an influential mode with painters. For artists such as Eva Švankmajerová, the focus of surrealism is the freedom of the individual, still highly relevant.

The Pilgrimage Church of Saint John of Nepomuk.

ARCHITECTURE

The earliest buildings in Bohemia and Moravia were made of wood. The oldest surviving buildings were built in the Romanesque style with thick walls, rounded arches, and large, closely spaced columns. From the thirteenth to sixteenth centuries, the Gothic style dominated public architecture in the Czech lands. Individual buildings, as well as town squares surrounded by arcaded houses built in that period, are still in use today.

In the early sixteenth century, the Italian Renaissance style developed distinct Czech touches, including stucco decorations of historical scenes. Good examples of the Baroque style of the early eighteenth century can be seen throughout the country. The Pilgrimage Church of Saint John of Nepomuk, built in 1720s in this style by Jan Santini Aichel, is listed as a UNESCO World Heritage Site. Its distinctive features include grand sculptures and frescoes, and gilded ornamentation. In the nineteenth century there was a revival of prior architectural styles—neoclassical, neo-Gothic, and neo-Renaissance.

Many beautiful hotels and cafés in Prague evoke that period. The communist era trampled creativity, leaving a legacy of ugly, massive, concrete public buildings and villages thrown together with prefabricated housing.

Many standing architectural treasures, however, are in need of restoration, and the government has set aside funds for their conservation. One of the more well-known modern Czech architects is Bořek Šípek (1949—2016), who was the architect of Prague Castle under the presidency of Václav Havel.

INTERNET LINKS

http://www.antonin-dvorak.cz/en/life/biography
This site provides a biography of Antonín Dvořák.

https://www.cmuse.org/six-most-interesting-facts-about -bedrich-smetana
A good overview of Smetana's life and accomplishments is posted on this site.

https://www.mucha.cz/en
This site of the Mucha Museum in Prague includes a biography and an overview of his works.

http://www.praguepuppetmuseum.com
The Prague Puppet Museum site is in English and includes photos.

https://theculturetrip.com/europe/czech-republic/articles/mapping -the-20th-century-a-journey-through-czech-art
This is an overview of twentieth century Czech artists, with photos and links.

http://whc.unesco.org/en/list/690
The UNESCO World Heritage site lists this entry for the Pilgrimage Church of St John of Nepomuk at Zelená Hora, as well as several other significant architectural works in Czechia.

LEISURE

A young girl prepares to harvest a large, edible wild mushroom in the Šumava National Park.

11

C ZECHS PURSUE A NUMBER OF activities for their enjoyment, from traditional sports and games to pastimes such as gathering mushrooms and berry picking or simply spending weekends at their country cottage, often gardening there.

SPORTS

Czechs have endless enthusiasm for many modern sports. Soccer is a national passion, and the country is often represented in the European soccer championship matches. Czechs also enjoy a national soccer competition. Young fans admire their favorite soccer heroes and collect photos of them.

Some Czechs say the national sport is ice hockey. Czechs have participated in European and world championships since the end of the nineteenth century. The Czech national men's ice hockey team is one of the most successful national teams in the world. They have won multiple World Championships, including the 2010 competition in Cologne, and took the gold at the 1998 Olympics at Nagano. In 2006, at the Turin Olympic Games, the team won a bronze.

Ice skating is also a favorite pastime. During the winter, when temperatures fall below freezing, sections of some parks are sprayed with water, converting them into ice rinks. Czechs also like to ski, and given the mountainous terrain of the country, there is a wide choice of slopes.

Mushroom hunting is a favorite pastime of the Czech people. Many townspeople spend weekends at their country cottages picking dozens of different fungi and feasting on them or preserving them for later use. In the late summer and early fall, Czechs take to the damp forests with a passion. On St. Václav Day in September, there are popular mushrooming competitions.

Tennis has an enthusiastic following, too. The Škoda Czech Open is held in early August in Prague. Famous Czech tennis players include Martina Navrátilová and Ivan Lendl. Both of those great players are now United States citizens.

Another favorite pastime is cycling in the countryside. The Czech landscape provides many varied and stunning locations, from the foothills of mountain ranges to the lakes in South Bohemia. Not many people cycle in the larger cities because of the predominance of cobbled streets, heavy traffic, and air pollution.

A mountain biker pedals up a dirt path in the woods.

A COUNTRY RETREAT

On the weekends, many Czech families head for their country cottages. The notion of a country retreat is a long-standing feature of Czech culture. These second homes may be heirloom cottages passed down through the family, cottages left vacant by people who moved to the cities, or newly built chalets on the edge of villages. Some cozy cabins are also available for short-term rentals.

After World War II, some three million Germans were forced to leave the Czech lands and return to Germany, abandoning their property. Czechs moved into the empty homes and possessed them by the simple process of occupying the buildings. During the communist years, when citizens were forbidden to express thoughts or beliefs contrary to the approved government policy, they would retreat to their second homes for some respite and honest conversation.

During the communist era country cottages were often in a state of extreme neglect and disrepair. More recently, people have begun to spend money renovating and restoring such properties. Czechs proudly refer to their "golden hands," noting that they are naturally adept at completing any manual task. Many happily spend the workweek planning what tasks they will tackle on the weekend, and assembling the right tools and materials.

THE SOKOL MOVEMENT

Physical education has a long tradition in the republic. A Czech professor of art history at Charles University, Miroslav Tyrs (1832–1884), founded an exercise movement called Sokol (meaning "falcon") in 1862. He was convinced that citizens needed to be of healthy mind and body in order to survive as a nation. Although the movement was based on a tradition of physical education through gymnastics and fitness training—stretching back to Renaissance times and earlier, the fifth century BCE in Greece—its role was essentially a cultural and political one, intended to inspire nationalistic pride in the people at a time when they were struggling for independence.

Part of the Sokol tradition involved rallies called slets *at which thousands of people would exercise in formation in a stadium, using banners and ribbons to present striking*

displays. Sokol members were targeted for abuse by the Nazis during the German occupation of Czechoslovakia in World War II and by the communists after the war, but Czechs held on to the robust tradition, fulfilling Miroslav Tyrs's vision of promoting nationalism. Sokol was revived publicly after 1989. The

movement spread abroad, including units in the United States and Canada. The most recent Sokol rally was held in 2012, but the movement no longer enjoys its previous popularity.

The 1997 and 2000 floods devastated many country homes. It took time to repair the damages, but the country cottage has continued as a treasured Czech tradition.

FREE TO TRAVEL

Recently, Czechs have become great travelers abroad. During the four decades under the communist regime, travel was not widely allowed, particularly to the West. Once the restrictions were lifted, foreign excursions became desired and realized vacations.

The most popular destination for many Czech holidaymakers has been the Croatian coast because of its sunny weather and good connections to and from the Czech Republic. Czech travelers often take frugal measures to save money and be self-sufficient. Many prefer to travel on a budget by taking their own food and supplies, including such Czech staples as sausages, beer, bread, canned meat, and dumpling mix. That makes them unpopular visitors in other countries, as they do not spend as much money as other tourists!

HEALING WATERS

Since Karlovy Vary was founded by Charles IV in the fourteenth century, many famous people have "taken the waters" at the spa towns in the Czech lands. The republic has many naturally occurring mineral springs, particularly in West Bohemia and North Moravia. Spa towns have developed where people go to treat medical conditions, usually by bathing in the mineral-infused waters or drinking it. West Bohemia spa towns include Karlovy Vary, Jáchymov, Františkovy Lázně, and Mariańské Lázně; in North Moravia a number of spa towns are located near the Jeseníky Mountains.

The spas specialize in treating one or more ailments—respiratory, thyroid, coronary, and rheumatic diseases; allergies; diseases of the liver, kidney, stomach, and skin are some of them. Elderly Czechs in particular enjoy taking the baths, whether to treat specific ailments or simply to relax in the thermal waters. Most spa towns are surrounded by magnificent countryside.

PARKS AND THE ARTS

Larger towns and cities usually have one or more public parks, and some feature formal gardens with carefully trimmed shrubs bordering arcaded walks. Czechs of all ages take advantage of these stretches of green for strolls, picnics, or a leisurely read under the fragrant magnolia trees. In summer, the parks are filled with people throwing Frisbees, playing guitars, walking their dogs, or quietly people watching.

A favorite leisure pursuit for older Czechs is the theater, especially opera. The arts have remained a constant factor in the lives of all Czechs. Those who have the time like to attend the many festivals and concerts offered in large cities. The concerts are not as inexpensive as they once were (under the communist regime, ticket prices were subsidized), but retired citizens are still entitled to lower ticket prices.

"The Singing Fountain" is a park feature in the spa town of Mariańské Lázně.

INTERNET LINKS

https://afocr.org/czech-sports
A history and overview of sports in the Czech Republic is provided on this page.

http://www.iihf.com/iihf-home/countries/czech-republic
This is the link for the International Ice Hockey Federation page for the Czech Republic team.

http://www.tresbohemes.com/2016/03/edible-wild-mushrooms
This is an article about hunting wild mushrooms in the Czech Republic.

FESTIVALS

People dressed in historical costumes walk in procession for the annual Five-Petalled Rose Celebration in Krumlov.

12

MOST CZECH FESTIVALS ARE colorful and fun. Many evoke a deep sense of history in a mix of Christian and pre-Christian rituals. Throughout the country, rites celebrating the seasons are held, varying in detail according to the region. Added to those are festivals of cultural and patriotic significance to Czechs.

Many of the festivals are celebrated in both cities and rural areas, while some are unique to certain locations. For some Czechs, a person's name day—the day of the saint for whom he or she is named—is as important, or even more so, as a birthday. Calendar companies publish lists of saints' days, and these help people to remember friends' name days with small gifts or cards. The name day custom is popular in many European Christian countries.

Hromnice (HROM-nyi-tseh), February 2, marks the midpoint between the winter solstice and the spring equinox. Just like Groundhog's Day in the United States, it predicts the end of winter according to folklore. "If the goose swims on water on Hromnice, it will walk on ice at Easter" is just one of many Czech sayings for the occasion.

CHRISTIAN TRADITIONS

Under the communist regime, the holy days of Easter and Christmas were work holidays, but their religious significance was downplayed by the government. Now these most important Christian holidays are celebrated with both religious and secular traditions.

Traditional Czech Easter eggs are red with white decorations.

EASTER The religious celebrations of Easter are integrated with pre-Christian rituals marking the change of seasons. The Sunday before Easter, Palm Sunday, is also a celebration of the arrival of spring. The figure of Death, made from sticks and cloth, is ceremoniously burned, representing the end of winter. Traditional Czechs decorate green branches with bright ribbons and eggs—symbolizing the cycle of new life—and bathe in springs believed to have a rejuvenating effect. In another Easter custom, beautifully decorated eggs are given away and also placed in house and shop windows. People also put other symbols of new life in their windows, such as pussy willow branches and dolls made of straw.

One spring ritual connected with Easter persists throughout the countryside: men and boys go around gently swatting women and girls with willow switches. In some places, they also pour buckets of water on women. These gestures are meant to represent fertility and seasonal rejuvenation, and they involve much merriment.

CHRISTMAS is a time for gifts, family, fun, and feasting, as it is elsewhere. Although its religious significance has dimmed considerably, the joyful rituals and delicious cookies and other foods associated with Christmas continue to be enjoyed by many Czechs.

On Saint Nicholas's Day, December 6, Saint Nicholas and the devil together visit the homes of family and close friends. (They are usually someone's father and uncle dressed up.) Saint Nicholas looks remarkably like the

A huge decorated tree glitters at the Prague Christmas Market in the Old Town Square.

Roman Catholic pope in a tall white hat and long white coat, and he carries a shepherd's staff. The devil wears a mask or heavy black makeup, horns on his head, an old fur coat, and sometimes a tail and a chain that rattles as he walks. Children who have been good receive a small gift such as fruit, nuts, or chocolate, whereas children who have been naughty are given a piece of coal.

Christmas Eve is also called Generous Day, and is special for its gift giving and traditional family meals. Dinner begins with carp soup, followed by carp either fried with breadcrumbs and served with potato salad, or served with black sauce. Dessert is a light fruitcake. Presents are opened with much enthusiasm after dinner. Some Czechs still like to go to midnight Mass.

Christmas Day is a family event. Lunch is traditionally roast turkey, dumplings, and sauerkraut. Adults may lift a glass or two of local wines or homemade brandies. The next day, Saint Stephen's Day, is spent recuperating. The Christmas season ends on January 6, the Day of the Three Kings, which is sometimes marked by carols and bell ringing.

January 1	Nový rok, *New Year's Day, is also the anniversary of the independence of the Czech Republic in 1993.*
March or April	Velký pátek, *Good Friday, became a national holiday in 2016.*
	Velikonoční pondělí, *Easter Monday.*
May 1	Svátek práce, *Labor Day, was important under the communist regime; it is now a day of enjoyment, usually spent picnicking in the countryside and often preceded by all-night revels.*
May 8	Den vítězství, *Liberation Day, marks the end of World War II in Europe in 1945.*
July 5	Den Cyrila a Metoděje, *Saints Cyril and Methodius Day, celebrates the introduction of Christianity and literacy to Slavs.*
July 6	Den Jana Husa, *Jan Hus Day, commemorates the burning at the stake in 1415 of the great theologian and religious reformer.*
September 28	Den české státnosti, *also St. Wenceslas Day, marks the day of Czech statehood.*
October 28	Den vzniku Československa, *Independence Day, marks the founding of the First Czechoslovak Republic in 1918.*
November 17	Den boje za svobodu a demokracii, *Struggle for Freedom and Democracy Day, commemorates students demonstrations in 1939 and 1989.*
December 24	Štědrý den, *Christmas Eve*
December 25	Vánoce, *Christmas.*
December 26	Den Svatý Štěpán, *Saint Stephen's Day*

BURNING OF THE WITCHES

This broom-burning festival, also called Witches' Night, is celebrated on April 30, and comes from a pre-Christian ritual to ward off evil forces. Witches (or those suspected of being witches) in particular were targeted, for they were believed to ride off on broomsticks to rendezvous with the devil.

A witch effigy is burned on Witches' Night to mark the end of winter.

In the Burning of the Witches ceremony, country people tidy their properties and gather on the highest hill for a ceremonial burning of their brooms as a symbolic defense against evil. Today the witches' occasion is also used to mark the end of winter and involves nighttime parties gathered around bonfires. There are also romantic customs for young couples—they jump over the dying embers together, and the next day the men lay branches with new leaves on the doorstep of their favorite girl.

STRÁŽNICE INTERNATIONAL FOLKLORE FESTIVAL

Since it was first held in 1945, the International Folklore Festival in Strážnice, Moravia, has played a key role in the preservation of traditional dress, music, and dance. Beloved national customs managed to survive during the years of cheerless communist rule even without official subsidies.

The festivities take place every last weekend in June in the park of a castle, with both organized and impromptu open-air musical performances, food stalls, and plenty of beer and wine. Festival highlights include a procession of costumed celebrants from all over Europe, which starts at the town's main square and makes it way to the castle park. Festivities continue into the night. Children and adults alike enjoy the occasion.

RIDE OF THE KINGS

A horseman takes part in the colorful Ride of the Kings celebration in Vlčnov.

In 2011, the Ride of the Kings celebration was inscribed on the UNESCO World Heritage list of the Intangible Cultural Heritage of Humanity. (The list marks traditions or "living expressions inherited from our ancestors and passed on by our descendants" that contribute to humanity's intangible cultural heritage.)

Only a few towns in southeast Moravia continue the tradition of the Ride of the Kings. This ritual takes place in the spring, usually May, as part of the observance of Pentecost (a Christian holiday). The festival celebrates the spring's new crops, and the ride itself relates to a young man's rite of passage, believed to harken back to an older European festival. Celebrating spring and new growth involves a lot of feasting accompanied by music and dancing. Intricately decorated folk dress is worn as part of the singing and dancing events.

For two days, the "king" recruits his court attendants, and then on Sunday they ride on horseback around town together to be accepted by the adult men. The king is usually about twelve years old. His helpers, however, may be up to eighteen years old.

The king holds a rose clenched between his teeth throughout the ceremony as he is not permitted to smile. He and his courtiers are dressed in women's clothing, which is a feature of an ancient ritual to protect the crops. The horses are decorated with ribbons and paper flowers. The ceremonial ride begins at the home of the king and winds its way through the village. Along the way, the helpers call out in verse, asking for gifts for the king, and onlookers respond by placing money in the helpers' boots. The celebrations end with a parade and more singing and dancing.

INTERNET LINKS

http://www.czechtourism.com/events
This tourism site describes holidays events in different parts of the country.

https://ich.unesco.org/en/RL/ride-of-the-kings-in-the-south-east -of-the-czech-republic-00564
This is the UNESCO listing for the Ride of the Kings.

http://praguemonitor.com/2009/04/23/burning-witches
A story about the Burning of the Witches is found on this news site.

https://www.ricksteves.com/europe/czech-republic/festivals
The major holidays and festivals are listed on this site, with links to certain events.

https://www.timeanddate.com/holidays/czech
This calendar site lists national and religious holidays in Czechia.

FOOD

Sweet pastry (staroměstský trdelník) 50 Czk

Trdelník, a traditional Czech pastry, beckons in a bakery window in Prague.

13

CZECH CUISINE FEATURES MANY similar dishes and flavors to its Central European neighbors: Austria, Hungary, Germany, Poland, and of course, Slovakia. For example, the traditional Hungarian goulash and German sauerkraut have become Czech staples. Czechs share the Slavic custom of flavoring foods with sour cream, paprika, caraway, onions, garlic, lemon, and vinegar. Fresh produce is not a large part of the Czech diet due to the cold Czech environment. The seafood that is available is largely fish that have been raised in artificial lakes or fish farms.

TRADITIONAL FARE

A typical Czech meal includes lots of meat and large portions of dumplings, potatoes, or rice covered in a thick sauce, accompanied by vegetables or sauerkraut. For their meat dish, Czechs prefer pork but like other meats, too. Poultry is roasted, whether chicken or the favorite—farm-bred goose. Stewed or roasted beef is served with the ever present dumplings and sauerkraut.

Czechs also enjoy preserved or pickled vegetables. Fresh vegetables, with the exception of salads, are not a regular dish in a Czech menu. Bacon, caraway seeds, and salt are typical flavorings. In the fall Czechs greatly enjoy the bountiful supply of a variety of mushrooms, which they pick on trips to the countryside.

As the republic is landlocked, seafood is generally not present on the dining table. Trout fished from mountain streams, however, is enjoyed by Czechs, as is carp from the ancient artificial ponds in South Bohemia. A feast with carp as the main dish is the traditional fare for Christmas Eve.

Bread is made in many styles, although rye bread is by far the most common, often flavored with caraway seeds.

Favorite snacks are smoked meats, cheese, or thick, spicy pork or beef sausages, which may be fried or boiled. The sausages are often served with mustard. Rye and wheat bread will often be served with cold meats and cheeses. *Bramboráky*, or potato pancakes, are also a typical fast-food snack.

Breakfast at home typically consists of bread with butter, jam, or yogurt; cheese; eggs; ham or sausage; and tea or coffee. Workers rushing off to work may stop at a small café, often equipped with a narrow counter or small, tall tables, which they stand around to quickly consume soup, rolls, and sausages. Some Czechs take sandwiches to work to eat during their morning break. Lunch is the main meal, but is usually a hurried affair, except on Sundays. When people can afford it, they go out for lunch and are always happy to enjoy a long break. Dinner will be a light meal and may consist of a cold buffet of meats and cheese with bread.

The kitchen is still very much a woman's domain. Many women prefer that their husbands stay out of the kitchen altogether and think nothing of spending several hours preparing the main meal without help. For a husband to wash the dishes is a very modern occurrence in most households.

A typical Sunday lunch usually begins with soup. It may be a light broth with savory pieces of bacon, vegetables, or noodles; a thick and heavy soup, such as potato with vegetables and mushrooms; or sliced tripe in broth with spices. The main course often consists of dumplings, sauerkraut, and roasted pork chops or goose. Other very common selections are roast beef and goulash, served with a dill cream sauce or mushroom sauce. A Czech specialty is roast beef served with lemon, cranberries, and bread dumplings in a sour cream sauce. French fries or rice may accompany the main course. Local beer, rather than imported soft drinks, usually accompanies every course of a meal.

DUMPLINGS AND DESSERTS

Dumplings are a common part of Czech cuisine. They are served with most main courses and are also made in sweet versions for dessert. Typical savory (meaning not sweet) dumplings are made with either a bread or potato base. *Kynute knedlíky* (KNED-liki; raised dumplings), which is made from milk, eggs, and yeast, rises like bread.

A traditional dish at Christmas lunch is bread or liver dumplings, the latter flavored with lemon zest and marjoram. A favorite sweet dessert is plum dumpling, where dried plums (prunes) are wrapped in a thin layer of dough, boiled, and then rolled in crushed poppy seeds mixed with cinnamon sugar. Fruit dumplings are a summer specialty, made not only with plums but also with blueberries and apricots, dripping with melted butter and served with cottage cheese.

Another favorite dessert with adults and children alike is *vanilkové rohlíčky*. This crescent-shaped cookie, made with ground almonds or walnuts, flavored with vanilla and dusted with confectioners' sugar, is served especially at Christmastime.

WHAT TO DRINK

A Czech usually offers a guest strong, sweet "Turkish-style" coffee. Hot water is poured over finely ground beans that end up as a paste at the bottom of the cup. Tea, which is not as popular as coffee, is commonly served with lemon. On a hot day, adults might choose beer.

Although Czechs are great beer consumers, Moravia is well known as a wine-growing region, especially in the southeast. A favorite pastime for friends and family is to gather at family-run wine cellars to taste wine and sing. A drink widely enjoyed in summer is white wine and soda water on ice. This seasonal mix is known in America as a spritzer. Czechs prefer hot wine in the winter.

Moravia is also famous for its fiery brandies, both plum and apricot, as well as cherry liqueurs. A popular drink all year-round is a mixture of rum and hot water in equal parts, flavored with lemon. The spa town of Karlovy Vary jealously guards the recipe to its locally produced spicy herbal liqueur, Becherovka, which is often served as an aperitif.

FAMOUS BEERS   Beer drinkers have a choice of a great variety of good beers, especially in Prague, for the home of Czech beer is Bohemia. The earliest record of the brewing tradition in Prague is a document dated 1082, while the famous brewing town of Plzeň (Pilsen) was allowed to produce its own beer in 1290. Czechs drink about 37 gallons (142.6 liters) per person each year—equivalent to more than 300 pint glasses of beer. In fact, Czechs drink more beer per capita than any other nation. The Czech Republic was the first country to have a beer museum as well as the first beer-brewing textbook.

In Bohemia beer accompanies most meals, including breakfast. Czechs drink beer the way Americans drink soft drinks. Beer is served almost everywhere except in wine bars. Most Czech beers are lagers, naturally brewed from handpicked hops—the flowery spikes of the hop vine—and contain between 3 percent and 6 percent alcohol. People like to drink their beer cold with a creamy head. Beer is known as *pivo* in all Slavonic languages.

Premium Czech beers such as Budvar and Pilsener Urquell are well-known throughout the world. Budvar, with its brewery in České Budějovice (Budweis), is the original Budweiser beer. One of Bohemia's oldest beers is the brand Regent, which has been in production since 1379. Bohemian beers are believed to be the best in the world because of the superior quality of Bohemian hops.

EATING OUT

Czech towns and cities have many different types of eating places, with the widest range of cuisines found in Prague. Czechs love to eat out and do so whenever their budget allows. A visiting friend is reason enough to have dinner at a popular restaurant or to step out for a beer at the pub.

In Prague alone, there are thousands of pubs and inns, some of which were established centuries ago. The historical pubs are now tourist haunts. Pubs serve food as well as beer, some of them running to roasts, goulash, sauerkraut—and, of course, dumplings. Wine bars usually sell snacks as well, and some serve full meals. The wines found in most bars are from Czech or Slovakian wineries.

Many Czechs frequent simple, self-service, cafeteria-style places, which offer soups and staples such as dumplings, sandwiches, salads, sausages, and goulash at reasonable prices. In Prague there is a tradition of elegant coffeehouses that serve coffee as well as numerous other drinks, except beer, and a selection of snacks and pastries. Recent innovations are bookshops with cafés or restaurants attached. Slovak-style rustic restaurants, which are found throughout the Czech Republic, typically serve barbecued chicken.

INTERNET LINKS

http://allrecipes.com/recipes/713/world-cuisine/european/eastern -european/czech
This recipe site of reader-contributed content has a selection of traditional Czech dishes.

http://www.seriouseats.com/2012/03/snapshots-from-prague-food -czech-republic.html
This slide show features ten "must-eat' dishes from Prague.

https://www.tasteofprague.com/pragueblog/traditional-czech-food -in-prague-what-to-have-and-where-to-have-it
Photos and descriptions of typical Czech foods are featured on this site.

HOVĚZÍ GULÁŠ (BEEF GOULASH)

¼ cup (60 milliliters) cooking oil

2 pounds (app. 1 kilogram) beef stew
    (chuck or round) cut into 1-inch
    (2.5 cm) cubes

2 medium onions, chopped

4 cloves garlic, chopped

2 teaspoons caraway seeds

Salt and pepper to taste

3 tsp sweet or Hungarian paprika

2 cups (app. ½ liter) chopped tomatoes in
    their juices

3 cups (705 grams) water

1 tablespoon beef base or 2 bouillon cubes

1 cup (150 grams) breadcrumbs (optional)

2 tsp dried marjoram

½ onion, chopped

Heat oil in a heavy Dutch oven or deep skillet on high heat. Add beef and brown on all sides. Lower heat. Remove beef and set aside.

Pour off excess fat, saving about 2 Tbsp (30 mL) in the pan. Add onions and cook over low heat, stirring occasionally, until softened. Stir in garlic, paprika, caraway seeds, salt and pepper, and cook 1 minute. Add beef, tomatoes, and water. Bring to a boil over high heat; stir in beef base or bouillon.

Cover the pan and lower heat so mixture is just simmering. Cook about 1 hour 45 minutes, adding more water if necessary to keep beef covered, or until beef is very tender.

Stir in bread crumbs, if using, and marjoram. Replace lid and cook over low heat until bread crumbs are absorbed.

Serve garnished with chopped onion. Serve with *knedlíky* (Czech dumplings) or boiled potatoes or noodles. Serves four.

VANILKOVÉ ROHLÍČKY (CZECH VANILLA CRESCENTS)

These are a favorite treat at Christmastime.

8 ounces (120 g) butter, at room temperature
5 Tbsp sugar
½ tsp salt
2 tsp vanilla extract
1 Tbsp water
2 cups (240 g) all-purpose flour
2 cups (240 g) almonds, walnuts, or hazelnuts,
   finely chopped
Confectioners' or vanilla sugar, as needed

Heat oven to 325 degrees Fahrenheit (165° Celsius). In a large bowl, cream the butter and then add the sugar, salt, vanilla, water. Mix until soft and creamy.

Add the flour and mix until smooth. Stir in the chopped nuts of your choice until completely incorporated.

Form walnut-sized pieces of dough into crescent shapes on parchment-lined baking sheets. Bake 15 to 20 minutes or until golden brown on the bottom.

Allow cookies to cool 2 minutes on the baking sheet. And then, while cookies are still warm, roll them in confectioners' sugar or vanilla sugar. Tap off excess sugar.

When cookies are completely cool, again roll in confectioners' or vanilla sugar. Tap off excess, and transfer to an airtight container. These will keep several weeks.

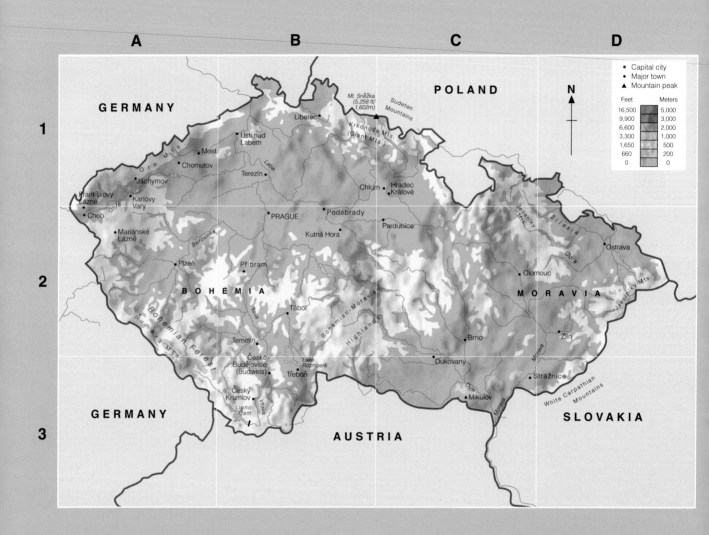

GERMANY

POLAND

Mt. Sněžka
(5,258 ft/
1,602m)

Sudeten
Mountains

Liberec

Krkonoše Mts.
(Giant Mts.)

1

Ústí nad
Labem

Most

Chomutov

Terezín

Labe

Jáchymov

Chlum

Hradec
Králové

Františkovy
Lázně

Karlovy
Vary

Cheb

Ohře

Jeseníky Mts.

Silesia

PRAGUE

Poděbrady

Pardubice

Mariánské
Lázně

Berounka

Kutná Hora

Odra

Ostrava

Plzeň

Příbram

Olomouc

2

B O H E M I A

M O R A V I A

Vltava

Tábor

Javorníky Mts.

Bohemian-Moravian

Highlands

Brno

Zlín

Temelín

Morava

Bohemian Forest

Šumava Mts.

České
Budějovice
(Budweis)

Lake
Rozmberk

Třeboň

Dukovany

Strážnice

Český
Krumlov

Vltava

Dyje

Mikulov

White Carpathian
Mountains

Lipno
Dam

GERMANY

AUSTRIA

SLOVAKIA

3

A   B   C   D

N

• Capital city
• Major town
▲ Mountain peak

Feet		Meters
16,500		5,000
9,900		3,000
6,600		2,000
3,300		1,000
1,650		500
660		200
0		0

MAP OF CZECH REPUBLIC

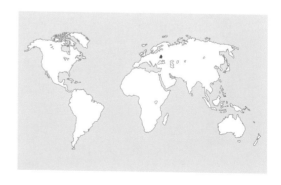

ECONOMIC CZECH REPUBLIC

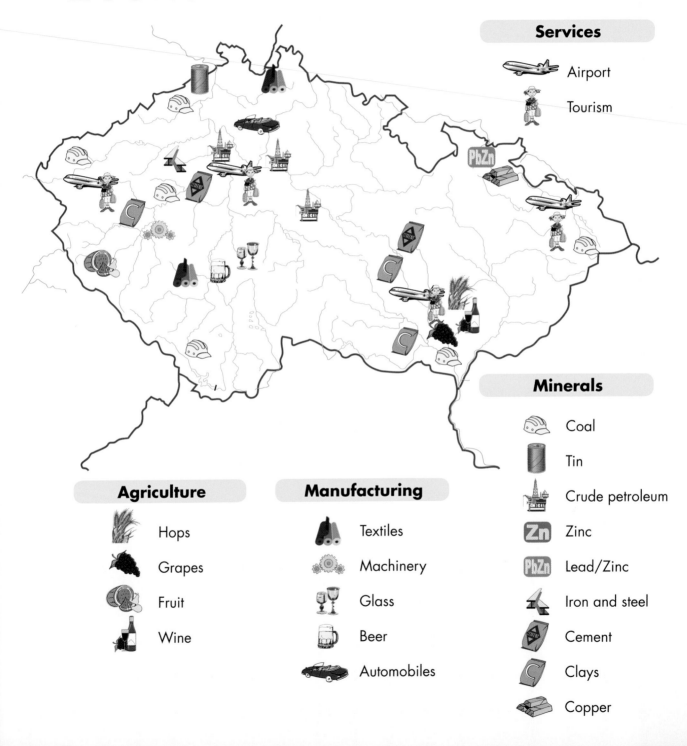

Services

- Airport
- Tourism

Agriculture

- Hops
- Grapes
- Fruit
- Wine

Manufacturing

- Textiles
- Machinery
- Glass
- Beer
- Automobiles

Minerals

- Coal
- Tin
- Crude petroleum
- Zn Zinc
- PbZn Lead/Zinc
- Iron and steel
- Cement
- Clays
- Copper

ABOUT THE ECONOMY

TYPE OF ECONOMY
Market economy

**GROSS DOMESTIC PRODUCT
(GDP, official exchange rate)**
$195.3 billion (2016)

GROWTH RATE
2.6 percent (2016)

INFLATION RATE
0.7 percent (2016)

CURRENCY
Czech koruna (Kč or, internationally, CZK)
USD1.00 = 21.76 CZK (November 2017)

MAIN EXPORTS
Machinery and transport equipment, raw
materials, fuel, chemicals

MAIN IMPORTS
Machinery and transport equipment, raw
materials and fuels, chemicals

MAIN TRADE PARTNERS
Germany, Slovakia, Poland, China, UK,
France, Netherlands, Italy, Austria

AGRICULTURAL PRODUCTS
Wheat, potatoes, sugar beets, hops, fruits;
pigs, poultry

INDUSTRIES
Motor vehicles, metallurgy, machinery and
equipment, glass, armaments

NATURAL RESOURCES
Hard coal, soft coal, kaolin, clay, graphite,
timber, arable land

LABOR FORCE
5.35 million (2016)

UNEMPLOYMENT RATE
4 percent (2016)

POPULATION BELOW POVERTY LINE
9.7 percent (2015)

CULTURAL CZECH REPUBLIC

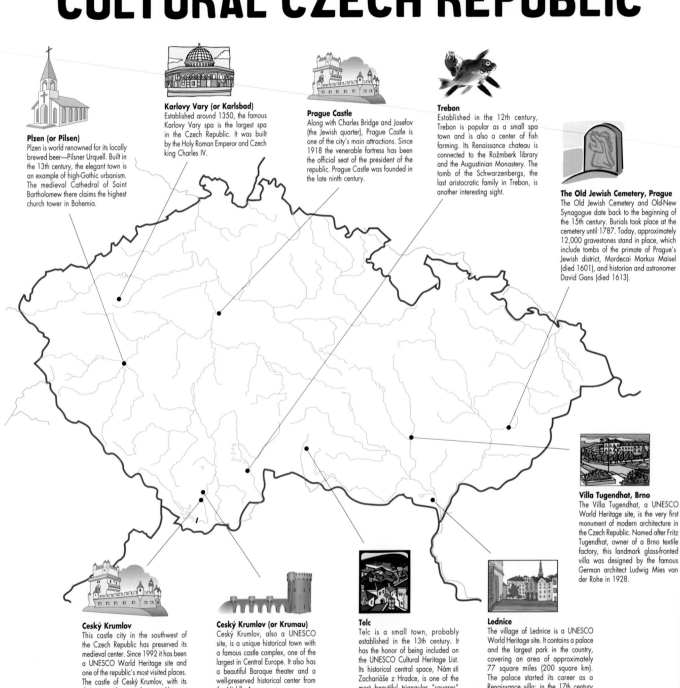

Plzen (or Pilsen)
Plzen is world renowned for its locally brewed beer—Pilsner Urquell. Built in the 13th century, the elegant town is an example of high-Gothic urbanism. The medieval Cathedral of Saint Bartholomew there claims the highest church tower in Bohemia.

Karlovy Vary (or Karlsbad)
Established around 1350, the famous Karlovy Vary spa is the largest spa in the Czech Republic. It was built by the Holy Roman Emperor and Czech king Charles IV.

Prague Castle
Along with Charles Bridge and Josefov (the Jewish quarter), Prague Castle is one of the city's main attractions. Since 1918 the venerable fortress has been the official seat of the president of the republic. Prague Castle was founded in the late ninth century.

Trebon
Established in the 12th century, Trebon is popular as a small spa town and is also a center of fish farming. Its Renaissance chateau is connected to the Rožmberk library and the Augustinian Monastery. The tomb of the Schwarzenbergs, the last aristocratic family in Trebon, is another interesting sight.

The Old Jewish Cemetery, Prague
The Old Jewish Cemetery and Old-New Synagogue date back to the beginning of the 15th century. Burials took place at the cemetery until 1787. Today, approximately 12,000 gravestones stand in place, which include tombs of the primate of Prague's Jewish district, Mordecai Markus Maisel (died 1601), and historian and astronomer David Gans (died 1613).

Villa Tugendhat, Brno
The Villa Tugendhat, a UNESCO World Heritage site, is the very first monument of modern architecture in the Czech Republic. Named after Fritz Tugendhat, owner of a Brno textile factory, this landmark glass-fronted villa was designed by the famous German architect Ludwig Mies van der Rohe in 1928.

Ceský Krumlov
This castle city in the southwest of the Czech Republic has preserved its medieval center. Since 1992 it has been a UNESCO World Heritage site and one of the republic's most visited places. The castle of Ceský Krumlov, with its distinctive red gate, is the second-biggest castle in Bohemia, incorporating over 40 buildings, 5 courtyards, and numerous parks. It took more than six centuries to complete the castle.

Ceský Krumlov (or Krumau)
Ceský Krumlov, also a UNESCO site, is a unique historical town with a famous castle complex, one of the largest in Central Europe. It also has a beautiful Baroque theater and a well-preserved historical center from the Middle Ages.

Telc
Telc is a small town, probably established in the 13th century. It has the honor of being included on the UNESCO Cultural Heritage List. Its historical central space, Nám stí Zachariáše z Hradce, is one of the most beautiful triangular "squares" in the republic.

Lednice
The village of Lednice is a UNESCO World Heritage site. It contains a palace and the largest park in the country, covering an area of approximately 77 square miles (200 square km). The palace started its career as a Renaissance villa; in the 17th century it became a summer residence of the ruling princes of Liechtenstein.

ABOUT THE CULTURE

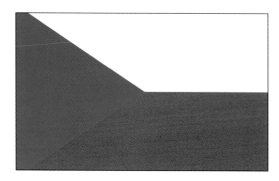

OFFICIAL NAME
Czech Republic

CONVENTIONAL SHORT FORM
Czechia

GOVERNMENT TYPE
Parliamentary republic

CAPITAL
Prague

AREA
30,450 square miles (78,866 square km)

POPULATION
10,674,723 (July 2017)

LANGUAGES
Czech (official) 95.4 percent, Slovak 1.6 percent, other 3 percent (2011 census)

ETHNIC GROUPS
Czech 64.3 percent, Moravian 5 percent, Slovak 1.4 percent, other 1.8 percent, unspecified 27.5 percent (2011)

RELIGIONS
Roman Catholic 10.4 percent, Protestant (includes Czech Brethren and Hussite) 1.1 percent, other and unspecified 54 percent, none 34.5 percent (2011)

INFANT MORTALITY RATE
2.6 deaths per 1,000 live births (2017)

LIFE EXPECTANCY AT BIRTH
Total population: 78.8 years
Male: 75.8 years
Female: 81.9 years (2017)

LITERACY
99 percent, male and female (2011)

TIMELINE

IN THE CZECH REPUBLIC	IN THE WORLD
1085	
Vratislav II becomes the first king of the Czech Přemyslid dynasty.	**1100** Rise of the Incan civilization in Peru
	1206
1306	Genghis Khan unifies the Mongols and starts conquest of the world.
The Přemyslid dynasty ends with the death of King Wenceslas III.	
1420–1434	
The Hussite Wars	**1558–1603** Reign of Elizabeth I of England
	1789–1799
1848	The French Revolution
The Czechs convene the first Slavic Congress.	**1869** The Suez Canal is opened.
	1914–1919
1918	World War I
Czech and Slovakia consolidate, establishing Czechoslovakia.	
1939	**1939–1945**
Czechoslovakia is invaded by Hitler's army.	World War II
1945	
Prague Uprising; the territories of the Czech Republic are liberated.	
1968	
Five Warsaw Pact countries invade Czechoslovakia; Soviet troops occupy the country until 1989.	**1969** Neil Armstrong becomes the first person to walk on the moon.
	1986
1989	Nuclear power disaster at Chernobyl in Ukraine
Velvet Revolution brings an end to communism; Václav Havel becomes president.	**1991** Breakup of the Soviet Union
1993	
Czechoslovakia splits into two countries.	
1997	
Václav Klaus government resigns. Caretaker government takes over.	
1998	
Václav Havel is reelected president.	

IN THE CZECH REPUBLIC	IN THE WORLD
1999	
The Czech Republic joins NATO.	**2001**
	Terrorists crash planes in New York, Washington, DC, and Pennsylvania.
2003	**2003**
Former prime minister Václav Klaus elected president.	War in Iraq begins.
2004	
Czech Republic joins the EU.	
2006	
Mirek Topolánek appointed as prime minister for the second time.	
2008	**2008**
Václav Klaus reelected as president; Czech Republic signs agreement permitting the United States to place part of its missile defense shield on Czech territory. Russia threatens to retaliate.	US elects first African American president, Barack Obama.
2011	
Václav Havel dies.	
2012	
New law allows for the Czech president to be elected by popular vote instead of being chosen by parliament.	
2013	
Former Prime Minister Miloš Zeman becomes president of the Czech Republic.	
2014	
Bohuslav Sobotka becomes prime minister.	
	2015–2016
2016	ISIS launches terror attacks in Belgium and France.
Czech parliament approves Czechia as the country's short form name.	
2017	**2017**
Andrej Babis is fired as finance minister over suspicions of tax evasion.	Donald Trump becomes US president.
	Britain begins Brexit process of leaving the EU.
ANO party wins parliamentary elections; Andrej Babis becomes the new prime minister.	Hurricanes devastate Houston, Caribbean islands, and Puerto Rico.

GLOSSARY

Art Nouveau
Art style of the late nineteenth and early twentieth centuries, characterized by flowing forms.

babička (BAB-ich-ka).
Grandmother

Bohemia
Geographical region in western Czech Republic.

Bohemian crystal
A famous type of crystal that has been cut in Bohemia for centuries.

Hapsburg (also spelled Habsburg)
Austrian-German dynasty that ruled the Czech lands from 1526 until 1914.

Hradčany
A castle and its environs in Prague.

Hussite movement/Hussites
Religious movement named after the theologian and reformer Jan Hus (1369—1415), whose followers were called Hussites.

knedlíky (KNED-liki)
Sweet or savory dumplings made from either a bread or potato base.

Moravia
Geographical region in eastern Czech Republic.

National Revival Movement
Czech nationalist movement in the late eighteenth and early nineteenth centuries, which saw the flowering of Czech literature, music, theater, and language.

Pan, Paní, Slečna (PAHN, PA-ni, SLE-tchna)
Mister, Missus, Miss—forms of address.

Prague Spring
A period in the 1960s under President Alexander Dubček when civil liberties were greater than had been usual under the communist regime.

sauerkraut
Sweet-sour pickled cabbage, a common dish reflecting German influence.

Silesia
Historical region found in the northeastern corner of the Czech Republic, as well as in Poland and Germany.

skansen (SKAN-suhn)
A Swedish term for an open-air museum of traditional architecture and furnishings.

Sokol
Exercise with banners and ribbons, performed by thousands of Czechs at rallies, often political.

FOR FURTHER INFORMATION

BOOKS

Albright, Madeleine. *Prague Winter: A Personal Story of Remembrance and War, 1937-1948.* New York, Harper Collins, 2012.

DK Eyewitness Travel. *Czech and Slovak Republics.* New York: DK Publishing, 2018.

Lonely Planet, Mark Baker and Neil Wilson. *Lonely Planet Prague and the Czech Republic*, 12th edition. Franklin, Tenn.: Lonely Planet Global Unlimited, 2017.

Zantovsky, Michael. *Havel: A Life.* New York, Grove Press, 2014.

ONLINE

BBC News. Czech Republic country profile.

http://www.bbc.com/news/world-europe-17220018

____. Czech Republic Timeline.

http://www.bbc.com/news/world-europe-17220571

CIA World Factbook. Czechia. https://www.cia.gov/library/publications/the-world-factbook /geos/ez.html

Czech Tourism. https://www.czechtourism.com

Encyclopaedia Britannica. Czech Republic. https://www.britannica.com/place/Czech-Republic

Lonely Planet. Czech Republic. https://www.lonelyplanet.com/czech-republic

New York Times, The. Czech Republic archives. https://www.nytimes.com/topic/destination /czech-republic

Prague Daily Monitor. http://praguemonitor.com

MUSIC

Dvorak: Symphony No. 9—From the New World, Op. 95 / Carnival Overture / Slavonic Dances Nos. 1 and 3, New York Philharmonic, Leonard Bernstein conductor, Sony Classical, 1998.

Folk Songs and Dances from Czechoslovakia. Smithsonian Folkways Records, 2004.

Jan Jirásek: Czech and Moravian Christmas Carols. Jitro Czech Children's Chorus. Navona, 2015.

Smetna, Ma Vlast. Czech Philharmonic/ Jiří Bělohlávek, conductor, Decca, 2018.

Song of a Czech: Dvorak and Janacek for Men's Voices, Cantus, 2013

BIBLIOGRAPHY

BBC News. Czech Republic Country Profile. http://www.bbc.com/news/world-europe-17220018

____. Czech Republic Timeline. http://www.bbc.com/news/world-europe-17220571

Bilesfsky, Dan and Jane Perlez. "Vaclav Havel, Former Czech President, Dies at 75." *The New York Times*, Dec. 18, 2011. http://www.nytimes.com/2011/12/19/world/europe/vaclav-havel-dissident-playwright-who-led-czechoslovakia-dead-at-75.html

CIA World Factbook. Czechia. https://www.cia.gov/library/publications/the-world-factbook/geos/ez.html

Czech Statistical Office. "Preliminary results of the 2011 Population and Housing Census." https://www.czso.cz/csu/sldb/preliminary_results_of_the_2011_population_and_housing_census

Encyclopaedia Britannica. Czech Republic. https://www.britannica.com/place/Czech-Republic

Eurostat. "People at risk of poverty or social exclusion by country 2008 and 2015." http://ec.europa.eu/eurostat/statistics-explained/index.php/File:People_at_risk_of_poverty_or_social_exclusion_by_country_2008_and_2015.JPG

Holy, Ladislav. *The Little Czech and the Great Czech Nation: National Identity and the Post-Communist Social Transformation*. Cambridge: Cambridge University Press, 1996.

Houston, Rebecca. "Czech's Dirty Word." Prague TV. October 17, 2007. https://prague.tv/en/s72/Directory/c206-Art-and-Culture/n1207-feminism-czechs-dirty-word

NěmeČková, Michaela et al., "Marriages and births in the Czech Republic." Eurostat, December 2015. http://ec.europa.eu/eurostat/statistics-explained/index.php/Marriages_and_births_in_the_Czech_Republic#Family_pattern_in_the_Czech_Republic_.E2.80.93_first_child_later_and_outside_marriage

Lincoln, Kevin. "15,000 People In The Czech Republic Say Their Religion Is 'Knights Of The Jedi'." Business Insider. December 19, 2011. http://www.businessinsider.com/czech-republic-jedi-2011-12

New York Times, The. Czech Republic archives. https://www.nytimes.com/topic/destination/czech-republic

Prague Daily Monitor. "Polluted air causes early death of up to 8,000 Czechs a year." January 12, 2017. http://praguemonitor.com/2017/01/12/polluted-air-causes-early-death-8000-czechs-year

United Nations Development Programme. Human Development Reports, Table 5: Gender Inequality Index 2016. http://hdr.undp.org/en/composite/GII

World Nuclear Association. "Nuclear Power in Czech Republic (updated 2017)" http://www.world-nuclear.org/information-library/country-profiles/countries-a-f/czech-republic.aspx

INDEX